FIRE
OF THE
GODDESS

About the Author

Katalin Koda is a passionate explorer of earth stories, women's mysteries and the mythic expression of our world. A practicing Vajrayana Buddhist, Katalin also works with indigenous wisdom and shamanism in her healing practice. She is a visionary artist, poet, and dreamer and has been teaching workshops on women's wisdom and spirituality, Reiki, shamanic journey and chakra healing for more than fifteen years. Please visit her website www.katalinkoda.com for more information.

KATALIN KODA

FiRE

OF THE

GODDESS

NINE PATHS TO IGNITE
THE SACRED FEMININE

Llewellyn Publications
Woodbury, Minnesota

First Edition
First Printing, 2011

Book design by Steffani Sawyer
Cover design by Adrienne Zimiga
Cover illustration by Kathleen Edwards

Llewellyn is a registered trademark of Llewellyn Worldwide Ltd.

Library of Congress Cataloging-in-Publication Data
Koda, Katalin, 1976–
    Fire of the Goddess : nine paths to ignite the sacred feminine / Katalin Koda. — 1st ed.
        p. cm.
    Includes bibliographical references.
    ISBN 978-0-7387-2003-6
1. Women—Prayers and devotions. 2. Goddesses—Meditations. 3. Spiritual exercises. I. Title.
    BL625.7.K64 2011
    204'.32082—dc22
                            2011009249

Llewellyn Publications
A Division of Llewellyn Worldwide Ltd.
2143 Wooddale Drive
Woodbury, Minnesota 55125-2989
www.llewellyn.com

Printed in the United States of America

*For all the women and girls of the world
who dare to leap, to shine brightly,
to love and dance and sing*

✦

CONTENTS

EXERCISES

INTRODUCTION

Be wild; that is how to clear the river.
—CLARISSA PINKOLA ESTÉS

We all come from a mother. We are born out of a woman, out of the womb—the small, dark, wet space that has no other purpose biologically but to carry life. Each one of us inhabits space: between our organs and within our lungs; in our nostrils to breathe and smell; in our ears so that we can hear the sounds of the world. Yet it is woman who holds the space to create life, to nurture it naturally for nine months, and to push it out into the world where that new life has the opportunity to grow and learn, dance and love, feel heartache and sorrow, channel spirit into form. This is an immense reality that can inspire us each and every day if we choose to pay closer attention to it. It is wondrous that every woman walks around with the great mystery of life dwelling within her.

For decades, women have been inspired to seek out new ways to relate to sacredness and honor the divine feminine. This is crucial to creating a more balanced view of the sacred, since most organized religions were originally written down by men and primarily constructed for male practice. This doesn't mean there is no wisdom in world religions, but the path of the woman, the spiritual capacity of a human that carries the creative force within, calls for a different way of approaching the sacred. Unlike traditional religious paths, contemporary women's connection to the spiritual comes in the form of ordinary reality. The number of women I know who are able to raise children in an expansive, holistic way as well as take care of the house and have a career (such as my own mother) is astonishing. We women should be applauding ourselves for our capacity to give birth, make a perfect cup of tea, and drum to the stars. We are limitless and we need to remind ourselves of that limitlessness on a daily basis.

Instead of transcending, the sacred feminine reminds us to simply be with what is, and celebrate it; to be with the messiness of birth; to celebrate each time our menses comes along; to sit quietly and respectfully with death; to honor our pregnancies, our years of breastfeeding, our times of going within and finding new aspects of the soul. The sacred feminine reminds us that even if we do not have children, we are still deeply connected to our mother and her processes; that we are a reflection of her power, her love, her wisdom. We are all a reflection of the beauty that is our earth and all her processes. Earth is our mother as much as our human mother and all things come from her and return to her, just as our bodies will one day decay in her soils.

Over and over and over again, I have read the story of the goddess: how she figured predominantly in the artwork of our ancestors for over 30,000 years. How she is the mother, weaver, dancer, lover, divine matrix, web builder, daughter, queen of heaven, queen of earth ... until her descent into the underworld some four to five thousand years B.C.E. The story of her loss seems to begin with Inanna/Astarte/Isis, and descend downward into the abyss beneath a patriarchal, kingdom worship of masculine divinity. Except for the phenomenon of Tantra that later arose in South India in 500 C.E., the predominant worship of the sacred feminine and the goddess was slowly crushed out of much of the world's religion, ideology, and philosophy and she was almost destroyed by the culture of the west.

We are now witnessing where the system of the past several thousand years has led us: rape and violence throughout the world, severe poverty, hunger and social unrest, unprecedented climate change and ecological destruction; meanwhile, we spend billions of dollars on space programs and seek to explain the mystery of the universe, often forgetting to solve our very real issues here on earth. But all of that is changing. Peoples' grassroots efforts are slowly gaining ground even if the the old system would have you think otherwise; there is no question now that the goddess—and all her guises of interconnectedness, immanence, and sacred feminine—is returning in full force. Even with all of the darkness of our history, we see that there is a light at the end of the tunnel. There is no stopping her. When the tide reaches critical mass, humanity will shift once again into a way of being that will be more connected with the earth. As I write this, Americans are hotly debating the need for universal health care. On the surface this may seem to be a political issue, but dig a bit deeper and you'll find that the crux of the issue is the our current capitalistic, dominant way of handling our health versus a system that supports people's well being. The anger and rage that is surfacing is a symptom of that shift. Even if the plan of universal health care fails this time, it will return, because as each of us wakes up to the immanence of the sacred feminine, we in turn affect and light the power of those around us.

This book provides women from all walks of life with a guided path to reclaim the divine, inner self by using sacred resources of indigenous knowledge. In simple, yet profound, work with archetypes, myth, and ceremony, women are encouraged to step out of the roles that no longer serve them and into a place that is embodied with power, love, and wisdom. The following pages give us the tools to claim our sacredness and transform our fears into power for healing—methods to connect with our deep wells of inner love and access our sacred and profound feminine wisdom.

My Own Path to the Sacred Feminine

When I first discovered the sacred feminine, I literally felt something inside my body change. My first breath of the sacred feminine came in the form of a high priestess of Wicca: honored as the dark starry night, the waxing and waning moon, the seas and elements. When I first experienced a full moon Wicca ceremony, I imagined myself drawing down the moon as the goddess or sacred feminine into my womb, the space inside that would always be just a space until my first pregnancy. I spent over a year intensely studying and practicing Wicca before moving abroad.

For nearly a decade, I lived in India, mostly in a village by the sea in the South, but also traveling and spending many months in the high Himalayas. In India the goddess is a living, breathing, sensual element of everyday life. The goddess is not a separate being, but is really just differ-ernt aspects of womanhood; each different deity symbolizes the different ways we relate to the world as women. My time in India taught me that the goddess is us eyeing ourselves in this world; that we, as women, are in the sacred form of the goddess, just as men are in sacred form of the god.

I was continuously inspired by goddesses such as the powerful war-rioress Durga, the goddess of motherhood; the poet Saraswati, who symbolizes art, music, and literature; and the wondrous goddess of the river, Ganga Ma. I reveled in the Indian women who lit a small flame every evening for the goddess and wore jasmine in their hair as an offering to the sacred feminine. I created ceremonies that were an eclectic mix of Wicca and Indian tantra, filled with power and magic. I began to claim myself and my being as a woman using the images of the sacred feminine as my guide. Along the way I had two miscarriages and two babies, one of whom died a few days after birth. I began to connect more deeply with women who had also lost babies to miscarriage, death, or abortion and felt a further kinship with the power of creating life within as well as the endings and honoring the cycles of life.

Over the course of many years, my studies grew to include the prac-tices of tarot, Reiki, Zazen (basic silent sitting and walking meditation), yoga, and Tibetan Buddhism, mainly Mahayana and Vajrayana teachings. I practiced the art of Reiki for over a decade and by doing the same simple practice repeatedly, I gained immense wisdom. I practiced many hours of Zazen over the course of an eight year period, which formed an impor-tant ground for my later teachings in visualization and deity practices of Tibetan Buddhism. All of these practices have informed my path differ-ently and I continue to incorporate them into my healing work. Diver-sity and cultivating different aspects of ourselves is an essential aspect of the sacred feminine, the part that enables us to create powerful ceremony, understand all the loving forms of our lives, and find wisdom in each multidimensional day.

Triple Goddess

The goddess is portrayed throughout various cultures and histories as a three-fold or triple-faced goddess. Contemporary Wicca practitioners, who practice crafting using the seasons, elements, and natural rhythms as guides, follow the cycles of the maiden or virgin, mother, and crone to guide their sacred ceremonies. This triple-fold view is connected to the three major times in a woman's life: before menses, the years of menses, and the time of and after menopause. This is reflected in the phases of the moon: new or waxing as the white goddess of birth and growth; full as the red goddess of love and battle; and old or waning moon as the black goddess of death and divination.[1]

After spending time working with these aspects of the goddess, I began to search further afield for varied expressions of the sacred feminine. These expressions are aspects of a wild, sacred feminine and resonate a very deep truth within our beings. This is not the feminine of gender, nor is it the feminine of biology, but the sacred feminine that connects us as human beings to life on this earth. I moved beyond the triple goddess into a nine-fold path that inspires us to access our own sacred feminine within.

The Nine-Fold Journey

When we focus our gifts and talents that are inherent to us as women, we are able to live from a place of authenticity, courage, and clarity. Using nine sacred archetypes, we unlock the rich natural resources within and develop our spiritual journey. The nine manifestations of the sacred feminine are Fire Bearer, Initiate, Warrioress, Consort, Healer, Bodhisattva, Priestess, Weaver, and Crone. Of course, there are many more aspects of the sacred feminine found both in cultures across time and space as well

---

1. Monica Sjöö and Barbara Mor, *The Great Cosmic Mother*, p. 97.

as within, but these are the nine I felt would be most accessible for women today. These nine archetypes are each associated with a specific goddess and one of her myths that will help to illuminate her role as the archetype. We can think of each of goddesses as an inspiration to activate our power, love, and wisdom as we develop on the path of the sacred feminine.

Besides the Crone, I have deliberately chosen nine archetypes that are functions in life, rather than biological roles. Although many women are mothers and wives, all are daughters and often sisters. I feel there are specific capabilities that are inherent to women, and are part of our being that enable us to move along the path of life in a way that is unique and empowering. For example, I use the archetype of the Healer, which is often found in women. Although we may only activate the Healer for ourselves and aren't necessarily becoming a literal healer, we are biologically wired to cultivate a natural inclination to think about the wellbeing of others. In the myths surrounding the patriarchy, the stories often revolve around the woman as a mother to a son, a wife to a husband, a daughter to a father. I specifically chose goddesses that can act as contemporary heroines and also honor woman in the roles of wild wanderer, creator, destroyer, guide, healer, and space-holder—roles that are inherent to women regardless of the men in their lives.

Power, Love, and Wisdom

The nine feminine archetypes naturally fall into three distinct categories: power, love, and wisdom. These themes are the three keys used in this book to provide a more balanced, empowered, clear, and motivated life; they are interdependent of each other and true activation relies on the three working together.

First, we work with power to bring in the energy that grounds us. Power provides us with the tools needed on our path and helps us to face and transform fears. When we become filled with power, we are better able to discern what is healthy for us, to know our own truths, and manifest our desires. The three archetypes that enable us to access our power are the Fire Bearer, Initiate, and Warrioress. The Fire Bearer gives us the fiery seed of new growth to open up to our inner sacredness. The Initate enables us to reclaim our past and transform darkness and pain into power and courage. The Warrioress empowers us further by giving us the tools to set clear boundaries and connect with our spirit animal guides.

Following power is love, where we activate nourishment for ourselves and others to find the well of deep healing and peace inside. Love is an action, a way of responding to the world with a measure of calm, peacefulness, and dignity. We access and activate our love through the three archetypes of Healer, Consort, and Bodhisattva. The Healer nourishes our soul, waters our freshly planted seeds of power, and shines her light onto our sprouting sacred selves. The Consort guides us towards activating our sexual life force energy as well as creating loving relations with others. The Bodhisattva, a being from the Mahayana Buddhist tradition who forsakes his or her own enlightenment until all beings become enlightened, is an embodiment of selfless service. The Bodhisattva inspires us to use love and compassion actively in our daily lives.

Anchoring power and love into wisdom is the final stage of the path. When we open ourselves to our inherent wisdom as women, we move into a place of sacred reverence that honors ourselves and our community. Wisdom gives us the opportunity to actively motivate others as we have been inspired along the path. The three archetypes that guide us into a place of wisdom are the Weaver, Priestess, and the Crone. The Weaver shows us how to find our inner wisdom by bringing together all the different aspects of ourselves and sharing them with the community. The Priestess guides us to stand in a place of wise leadership, to use our gifts that we have discovered along the way and inspire other women to find their inner sacredness. Finally, the Crone, the ancient wise woman, shows us the importance of passing on wisdom, honoring the ancestors, and accepting endings and dissolution.

How to Use This Book

This book is designed for women who want to connect with sacredness but are not sure how, and for expanding the work of more advanced practitioners. First and foremost, before you begin to work with the contents of this book, I encourage you to cultivate some level of body awareness.

Many of us are extremely busy, rush about all day long, and come home to numb ourselves with wine, television, or the Internet. Before we know it, months and even years have passed us by without an awareness of our deeper needs. By simply tuning into our bodies and to what is available to us in the here and now we can become more centered and balanced. I recommend simply focusing on your breath every day for at least five minutes (see Chapter Six, Exercise 6.1 for a more detailed explanation of how to focus on your breath). If you cannot find five minutes a day to simply breathe and sit with yourself, then I guarantee that there is a strong possibility that something in your life is out of balance. It is no secret that meditation, yoga, and breath work is extremely beneficial to your health and peace of mind.

I also encourage you to connect to the rhythms of your womb, as this is an immediate way to access the sacred feminine. By paying attention to your monthy cycle, you will gain a stronger connection to your own spirituality. Pay attention to the current moon cycle each time you have your period. Is it new or full, waxing or waning? All creatures on earth, as well as the tides of the ocean, are affected by the changing moon cycles. It is not a coincidence that humans have honored the moon and her rhythms for thousands of years. Both the moon cycle and your menstrual cycle have a direct effect on your emotions as well as on the intuitive gifts that are naturally enhanced during this time. Even if you have passed through menarche, you still have a strong connection to the moons and rhythms of the seasons. We have been trained to turn off the awareness of our breath, our bodies, and our periods for far too long, and I strongly encourage you to bring back that awareness.

As we cultivate body awareness, we can begin to work with the tools of the sacred feminine. Each of the following nine chapters contains an archetype, a goddess associated with that archetype, a myth about the goddess, exercises to work with her, and a ceremony to connect to the archetype. Even if you have never created a ceremony, an altar, or even felt drawn to work with goddesses, I encourage you to be open to the ideas presented here. These methods have been used for millennia by indigenous peoples to find harmony with themselves and with the earth. They are very simple yet powerful ways to connect to who we are as women, to feel a connection to our earth, and to share our gifts and talents with our communities. Although I have included advanced terminology in some of the ceremonies (and an appendix to explain these), I recommend that you try working with these tools as a way to enhance the sacredness of your life.

Tools of the Sacred Feminine

The first tool of the sacred feminine is the archetype which is associated with a particular goddess. Archetypes are collective forms or universal imprints that reside in each of us such as the mother figure, lover, healer, and priestess. I have chosen specific goddesses to represent nine feminine archetypes, although there are many more. For example, Isis, an ancient goddess of Egypt, symbolizes the priestess archetype. We can think of the goddesses as divine aspects of the feminine universe which inevitably reside within us. When we choose to work with sacred forms such as goddesses, we are choosing to reprogram our mind to align with greater forces that have a positive impact on our well being. For example, we may find that we obsess over something or are filled with anxiety and doubts. By focusing on the image of Quan Yin, the goddess of peace, tranquility, and compassion, we are choosing to embody aspects that are more nourishing to our well being. This does not require that we worship them, or even give up our own beliefs to use these goddesses. They are simply forms that help us to cultivate a more positive and healing mind. When our mind relaxes, many of our worries drift away and it becomes much easier to create peace in our daily life as well as feeling more healthy and fulfilled.

We can imagine each of the nine goddesses or archetypes as seeds that, over time, will grow different qualities that will help us to create more sacredness in our daily lives. Although the nine aspects of the sacred feminine follow a natural progression from one development to another, you can use them in any order you wish. You may want to work with each archetype for a set amount of time, such as a week or month. This will give you a chance to really explore the deeper meanings of each goddess, allow them to come and speak to you in your dreams and subconscious, and give you time to practice the ceremony at the end of each chapter.

Each chapter begins with a short visualization to get you in touch with the archetype. I recommend that you take a moment before starting each chapter to light a candle and focus on your breath before reading the powerful visualization. This will help you to construct a mental and emotional connection between yourself and the archetype you will be exploring. This also enables you to help access your subconscious more fully.

The next sacred feminine tool is myth. In the following chapters, you will find that I have chosen a myth or story that clearly illustrates each of the archetypes. Myths are epic stories that hold keys in the form of archetypes to aid us in understanding the bigger, more powerful events of our own lives. Although we may not realize it, each of us harbors a collection of inner stories and it is these stories that often dictate who we are and why we make certain choices. For example, if we identify as a daughter, we may act out in certain ways we believe daughters are supposed to behave. When we examine our inner stories, we can begin to make choices about which myths we choose to embody. Many of us are filled with stories that the media has pumped into us without our awareness. If we are to examine the stories we are being told by the mainstream media, we find that many of them still portray women as passive wives, hardworking mothers, or obedient daughters. By reexamining our roles, we can start asking ourselves how we may limit our lives and how we can transform beliefs that no longer serve us into a more powerful, loving and wise self.

This book provides several different kinds of stories that seek to empower our inner sacred feminine. Myths help guide us in major life changes, trials, and various obstacles. In the Initiate chapter, there is the story of Inanna, a goddess of ancient Sumeria, who journeys into the darkness, surrenders her body, dies, and is then reborn as whole once again. This story not only inspires our conscious mind, it seeds our subconscious with a transformative key that helps us face our own darkness—such as loss, divorce, or illness. Reading and contemplating the myths in this book and using them as inspiration will help you to create powerful new stories that honor the power, love, and wisdom that we hold as women.

The myths have been shortened to make them more accessible, but if you feel called to explore them further, the resource list in the back of the book can help direct you to the longer versions of these stories. When you read the myths, I encourage you to take your time and visualize the imagery. You can choose to record the myth and play it back or have someone read it aloud as a way to further engage with the images and story that is being told. This way, you will plant worthy seeds into your subconscious, seeds that speak of power, love, and wisdom that comes in the shape of the goddesses featured in each story.

Once we have begun cultivating body awareness, studied archetypes, and contemplated inspiring myths, we can then work with the next tool, ceremony or ritual, to further embody the sacred feminine. Creating ceremony is the process of setting an intention and then using a form to encapsulate that intention, thus making it more powerful. Ceremony works as a symbolic language to feed our soul; it is the sacred technology that makes contact with our subconscious self, enables healing and transformation, and activates the deep forces of power, love, and wisdom within. For example, we may want to manifest certain things in our life. By manifesting an intention, then planting a seed as a symbolic gesture of change, we are effectively communicating to our subconscious that we are taking actions to welcome that intention into our lives. This is far more powerful than haphazardly wishing for things to happen to us. Another way ceremony can assist us is the honoring of passages in our life at times of change and transformation. Included in this book are ceremonies to help you honor your own major life changes including reclaiming your first menses and a croning ceremony for experiencing menopause.

By creating ceremony we relinquish our smaller self and merge with the dynamic, larger spirit; we are dissolving our ego and habitual tendencies into the connectedness of the universe. Each time we create ceremony, we become more fluid and less attached to stagnant emotions and mental constructs. We are revitalized by the wonder of our universe. This is why tribal cultures create spontaneous ceremony; this is why people love to dance, make music, and create art: to repeatedly dissolve the smaller self is to provide continuous, spiritual nourishment. I have found that when I create ceremony every month, it is as if my life becomes dotted with the seeds of light. Instead of a monthly stream of mundane activities, there are dots of brilliant light woven into my everyday world. With time, this light spills out into all of my days and infuses the mundane tasks of cooking, cleaning, and caring for my child in a sacred way.

Some of the ceremonies and exercises will be appropriate for you and some will not. They are there to try and see what sticks. Simply change or throw out what doesn't work; these are only guidelines to create a more sacred and fulfilling existence. There are ceremonies for single women and groups, and your own spontaneity and creativity are encouraged. There are several exercises which include various ways to connect with your own sacred feminine—including how to reclaim your menstruation, cultivate intuition, and honor your life as a woman—which can be also woven into ceremony if you wish. Remember that ritual and ceremony are sacred technology that heals, enables us to understand our life purpose, and reconnects us with our inner sacred feminine.

Working with the Elements

Part of the sacred feminine path is working closely with the elements. Traditionally, cultures have used the four primary elements of earth, fire, water, and air to create sacred space, make ceremony, enhance visualizations, and perform magic. Some traditions also include the elements of above (sky), below (mother earth), and center or space. As we work through the book, the elements will be discussed and used in the exercises and ceremonies.

Traditionally each element has certain qualities, colors, and associations. In some of the ceremonies in this book, I have suggested certain elements and offerings in connection with the directions. However, this book is not about working with a specific tradition and I encourage you to develop your own relationship with each element. You can discover your personal connection to earth, fire, water, and air by simply writing down your associations and then drawing them on paper. Sit with four blank pieces of papers, write "Earth" on the top of the first one, and write a list of what you associate with earth. Just let it flow without trying to analyze or judge. Then using crayons, pastels, paints, or other art supplies, draw images of what you relate to each of the elements. Do this for each element. This way, you will begin to dialogue with the elements. Also notice the elements and how they work in the natural world around you: how the fiery sun rises in the morning, the earthiness of the soil and rocks, the water of rain or snow, and the air in the wind and breezes. These elements are reflected in your body as well: the fire of digestion, the earthy quality of bone and muscle, the water in your mouth and tears, and the air of your breath moving in and out of your lungs. We can find these elements, along with the space of our body cavities, our nose and mouth, and our wombs, woven into each aspect of living.

Setting Solid Ground

Before continuing with the rest of the book, learning the myths, and using the exercises, it is important to set a solid ground for your practice. These three crucial steps are essential to creating ceremony effectively. These steps are the beginning of bringing sacred awareness into our everyday life. Each of the steps below can be extremely simple or more complex. For example, when you create an altar, you can make a small shelf in your home, or you may have an entire room devoted to sacred space and precious objects. This is up to you and what you can easily manage. The idea is to simply begin seeding your life with a level of sacredness. A good rule of thumb is to keep it simple. If your own altar is overwhelming you, then that could be a sign that you are trying too hard.

Creating an Altar or Shrine

This is the first step to effectively working with the sacred feminine. This involves creating a sacred space somewhere in your home or garden. Traditionally, cultures use altars as a place to give offerings to the spirits; later it became a more formal place in religious activity. However, we do not need to follow such a formal method. You can start by simply clearing off a shelf, covering it with a colored cloth, and placing a few items that you love such as a picture of your grandmother, a rock or nest or shell that you found, or an image of a deity or symbol that you feel drawn to. Think of this like a mini art project where you are allowing your subconscious to communicate through your altar. By creating a space of sacred objects that speaks to your soul you open up a dialogue between your conscious and unconscious mind. I encourage you to use aspects of the elements (a candle for fire, incense for air, a stone for earth, a bowl of water, for example), images, cards, natural objects, flowers, feathers, precious objects, and anything else that you may feel connected to. Change the items on your altar as often as you wish. You may wish to use your altar as a reflection of the seasons, yearly changes, and moon cycles. For example, put colored leaves on your altar to symbolize autumn and a time of letting go or going within.

Making Offerings

Every day we consume and use resources from the earth—from our food to our clothing, home, car, laptop, etc. We can forget that we are consistently using the earth and a good way to remind ourselves of this fact is to give something back to the earth. Indigenous cultures think of the earth not as a mass of resources but as a living entity or mother who provides nourishment to her children; our planet is an example of a powerful form of generosity. When we cultivate a practice of giving offerings, we are connecting ourselves to the earth and the living things around us, feeling a sense of gratitude or thankfulness for our sustenance. This helps us to open our hearts and to cultivate a more peaceful way of relating to each other. When we give offerings on our altar or sacred space, we can offer to the earth in general, or sometimes we can be more specific and show gratitude toward certain people in our lives, the food we eat, or the abundance that exists in our world. This also helps us to recognize that our lives often have many wonderful components in them and help loosen any anxiety we may feel over not having enough. Our offering can be as simple as a flower, a bowl of water, or a grain of rice. The point is to simply perform the action as a symbolic message to our subconscious to open our heart in thankfulness. Traditionally, specific offerings are given for each of the directions and the elements associated with those directions. I have listed those below. This work can easily be cultivated into a weekly or daily practice such as refilling a water bowl each morning as an offering to the earth or spirits or your family. All over the world people still practice this art and I encourage you to reconnect with this simple work; you will experience immediate benefits.

Calling in the Circle

After you prepare an altar and have worked with offerings, you will be ready to call a circle, which is the first step in creating ceremony. When you call a circle, you are creating a container for your ceremonial work; this intensifies both the experience and the magic at work. To call a circle, stand in each direction and call that direction. Then visualize a brilliant ring of light encircling you and whoever is participating the ceremony with you. The intention is to create a safe and sacred space which allows your connection to your spirit and subconscious to be intensified.

Throughout this book, I have included the calling of seven directions: the four cardinal directions, above, below and center. You may simplify this and only use the four cardinal directions or you may use all seven. Use your element association list and images to build your personal connection to the elements each time you create a ceremony. Usually, directions are called clockwise, starting perhaps with east or south (although you can choose to start with any direction you wish). If you start in the east, then follow with south, west, north, below, above, and center. I loosely associate the directions with the following elements: east with air; south with fire; west with water; north with ancestors/stones and bones; below with mother earth; and above with father sky. When you call a direction, you will want to call both the direction and the element, as well as give an offering. You may say something like, "I call the east, the element of air. Remind us that every breath is sacred..." and then offer incense or a feather; repeat this with each element: offer a candle or embers for south, water for west, and a crystal for the north. Mother earth is the below who nourishes us through all her gifts and father sky is above us who provides us wisdom and the long past and future. The center is ourselves, actively holding the central focus between the four directions, channeling the earth and sky. Feeling the space, the center of creation within your body, is a nice way to connect your body directly to the circle. The center, like our womb, goes with us everywhere. You may find your own way of honoring these directions and/or simply calling a circle.

Once you have called the directions, visualize a brilliant circle of light surrounding you, the other participants, and the space where you will do your ceremony work. Make sure to imagine the circle large enough to hold everyone in it as well as your working space. The purpose of the circle is to provide a container, which is then infused with potent energy. This sends a message to your subconscious, activating a more focused energy into your ceremonial work.

After you complete each ceremony, make sure to also close the circle. This is very important and I cannot stress this enough! I have attended too many ceremonies where circles are cast, energy is raised, and then all our good work is dissipated by not properly closing the circle. This is also important to not only follow through on our practice, but to really feel a solid sense of gratitude for all that we have. When we close the circle, it can be a very simpleaction, but focused by simply thanking and releasing each of the directions and/or elements. You can do this by saying something like, "East, we thank you for your presence. We honor the air and sacredness of breath." You can release each element in the same order or backwards, starting with the last direction called in. This often has a more releasing feel to it.

A Note on Ceremony Work

Each chapter contains a ceremony that reflects the archetype and goddess discussed in that chapter. The ceremonies are somewhat elaborate and include detailed instructions on how to work with various energies and cycles of our lives. If you are a beginner to this kind of work, feel free to either omit aspects of the ceremony that you do not understand or resonate with and/or research what is unfamiliar. For example, I may mention to use an oracle such as the tarot or runes at a certain part of the ceremony. If this is entirely unfamiliar for you, then simply omit that part for the time being and then, perhaps, research oracles and see if there is one that resonates with you to use in the future. I have included an appendix in the back of the book which explains various terms and tools that are referred to in the ceremonies. None of these ceremonies are set in stone and the essential qualities for each are your intention and creation of a form to more fully connect your conscious mind to your subconscious spiritual self. You may also wish to change, rearrange, or substitute aspects of the ceremonies to more fully suit your needs. The idea behind creating ceremony is to bring sacred art into your daily awareness so that you can more fully celebrate your life and open up to the power, love, and wisdom that inherently belong to you.

ONE

THE FIRE BEARER
Igniting the Inner Fire

*And the day came when the risk to remain tight in a
bud was more painful than the risk it took to blossom.*
—ANAÏS NIN

*Imagine you are standing on a cliff facing the ocean; the
waves are crashing, and the air is sweet and salty. The sun
is rising directly in front of you as the stars above slowly fade
into the lightening sky. You turn and look behind you. There
is a river of molten, fiery lava oozing down the mountain-
side making its way to the ocean. The lava drips into the
sea, the primordial life energy meeting the turquoise waters.
It is so hot that it continues to flame in the brilliant cooling
water. When the two forces collide, huge clouds of vaporous
steam rise out of the mixture, illuminated by the glowing
light of the lava. You stand with a sense of awe watching the
fire, water, and steam. This is a moment of utter paradox
in which old land is destroyed and new land is created. You
take a deep breath, open your hands and heart, and close*

your eyes. Suddenly there is a massive explosion and lava spews out in front of you, embers fall around you but do not harm you. One ember lands in your outstretched hand. This is a seed of light, a gift from the sacred earth in the form of the Fire Bearer. You take this seed of light in reverence and gratitude. You know, in that moment, you will plant the seed and cultivate your own sacred feminine just as the lava creates new earth.

The Fire Bearer is the first archetype we meet on the path of the sacred feminine. She is the gift that inspires us to give birth to a life imbued with power, love, and wisdom. The Fire Bearer symbolizes the seed of our inner light and holds the powerful potential to grow a sacred existence. The Fire Bearer comes to us as Pele, the fiery goddess who is believed to live in the Halema'uma'u crater of the volcano Kilauea on the Big Island of Hawai'i and who presides over the active lava flow.

The work of the Fire Bearer is both creative and destructive. When we begin the deep work of healing and transforming our pain, we recognize our inner creative power and destroy what no longer works for us. Creative passions come in the form of birthing children, making art, or creating a new way of living. Destroying the old may come in the form of leaving home, divorce, or simply letting go of old stuff. As molten lava creates new land on the island of Hawai'i, it also destroys whatever is in its path. This is one of the potent messages of the Fire Bearer: to step boldly, create new life, and remain fearless as we destroy what no longer works.

The Fire Bearer becomes apparent in our lives when we realize we are the keepers of a precious gift. This gift may be a talent or special skill such as healing, singing, or writing. This gift can also be our capacity to experience love, connectedness, beauty, truth, and joy. Coming to this realization is so simple, yet vital; it is akin to realizing the preciousness of our very own breath and body.

Recognizing the Sacred Land

When I arrived in Hawai'i, I felt a strong connection to the goddess Pele and her creative and destructive power. Because I live in a place that could be destroyed by lava at any moment, I am constantly reminded of the power of nature. Pele as Fire Bearer shows us that we must honor our surrounding environment. We cannot fully appreciate our own creative gifts until we deeply connect with the earth and know that our fiery spirit is manifest on this planet, right here and now. The Fire Bearer is presenting us the seed of this reality, to recognize our gifts within and without. It is up to us to cultivate that seed into a blaze of creative energy. No matter where we live, the nature around us is full of life and power and has the capacity to inspire our own fire. In the path of the sacred feminine, we can look more deeply at our own surroundings and find her presence, thus honoring our earth more deeply.

My own connections to the sacred feminine are inspired by living in India and Hawai'i, where goddesses are still worshipped and reverence for the sacred feminine is a living tradition. Much of the ancestral knowledge is still intact along with the stories that connect the people to the land. Everywhere I travel in both India and Hawai'i, ancient stories are told about the land: a giant stone perched on a desert mound is Krishna's cosmic butterball; glistening lakes in the desert are where Sita's tears fell when she was abducted by the demon king of Ceylon; on the island of Kaua'i of the Hawai'ian islands, Pele dug with her digging stick, leaving behind a lava hill called Pu'uopele (the hill of Pele); near my home on the Big Island of Hawai'i is the cave, referred to as the yoni cave today, and the flying vagina cave in ancient Hawai'ian story. Seeing the perfectly formed vulva of hardened lava in a cave was a wondrous experience that deeply nourished my feminine spirit.

I am continuously enchanted by these stories that have woven into the culture for thousands of years. When I arrived in Hawai'i, I felt compelled to give many offerings to Pele as well as other gods and goddesses, such as Kanaloa of the sea. Pele in turn showed me the gift of the Fire Bearer, which was the seed for this book. Finding out about your own land and its stories will help you connect to your inner Fire Bearer, thus opening the way to journey the sacred feminine.

Seeking Out a Local Goddess

Just as I connected with Pele upon my arrival in Hawai'i, I encourage you to connect with a goddess or heroine who existed in your neighborhood, state, or area of the country. The Fire Bearer archetype reminds us that seeking out stories that nourish us will activate our own inner creative fire. Go to the library and research which native peoples lived where you now live and who were the heroines, goddesses, or warrior women. If you cannot find a story from the distant past, then search for a story of a woman who lived in your area more recently, a story that compels you. Reclaim her stories and then connect her to the landscape around you.

Research the geography, the plants, the trees, and other natural aspects of the place where you live. See if you can find any folktales containing herbal remedies, older wisdom, and interesting stories that are still floating around the locale. Digging down into the ancestry of a place will naturally connect you more deeply with it. Similarly, learn the plants and trees of your neighborhood, find out which herbs and fruits grow locally. Identifying and eating local foods will help your body resonate more clearly with the elements and natural world that surrounds you.

This exercise also gives you an opportunity to create a link to the spirits of a place, the place you are choosing to reside. Perhaps you can think more carefully about this land you live on, not only the plants and trees surrounding you, but other natural formations as well. What are the water sources nearby? Are you close to the ocean, or to any rivers or streams? What kinds of forests are within walking or driving distance? What do these natural formations feel like? Even under slabs of cement, the living, breathing earth is there. You may feel drawn to act as a more conscious steward of your living earth home by cleaning up the river you meditate by; planting flowers and herbs in the patch of bare soil near your apartment building; sitting in the moonlight in the park with friends to make ceremony and help heal the crimes that may have been committed there.

Pele

Pele is the Fire Bearer who brought her magic fire-making stick and powers to the Big Island of Hawai'i many thousands of years ago. Looking at a satellite image, we can see the gorgeous green and yellow of the jungle surrounding what looks like a red, pulsing vagina, a massive opening in the earth that is continuously birthing molten lava, simultaneously destroying and creating new land. Pele's presence is powerful and her mythology survived both the Christianization of the Hawai'ian islands as well as its induction into statehood. Numerous stories and chants about Pele have been passed down for hundreds of years. Each year several *hula halau*, hula schools, perform at the active crater on Kilauea. Pele is respected, feared, and honored on the island.

During a journey meditation, I visited Pele and asked her for a vision for this book. She gave me a small, glowing ember, like a seed, which holds the potential to build a great fire; thus I recognized her as Fire Bearer. My role was to receive this fire and allow it to grow within me. Just as a seed has the potential to become a tree or flower and produce countless more seeds, an ember has the ability to produce countless fires. This mirrored the potential of the Fire Bearer, of the path of the sacred feminine: to recognize the seed of power which can spread outward to others. This ember glowed symbolically as both the beginning and ending of a cycle. Like the Crone, the Fire Bearer holds the power of destruction; yet from those ashes come the incredible seeds of creativity. This ember is like the seeds we plant at the new moon, seeds that grow plants or children or new projects.

How Pele Came to Live on Hawai'i[2]

Pele was born with long flowing red hair, different from all the rest of her dark-haired brothers and sisters. Her temper was quite fierce, another trait that set her apart from her family. Pele's mother was the earth goddess Haumea and her father was Wākea, ruler of the sky. She had many brothers and sisters, all guardians of the elements of nature. Pele inspired love and devotion in all of her family except for one sister, Nāmakaokaha'i, or Nāmaka, the goddess of water, who was threatened by Pele's fiery nature.

As a child, Pele loved to lick the fire and dance with the flames. This sickened her sister Nāmaka, who would watch from the outskirts as Pele's scarlet hair caught fire and she inhaled cinders delightedly. Nāmaka knew Pele carried immense power, holding the potential to burn bigger and brighter than any fire. Once when Pele realized Nāmaka was watching her, Pele shrugged and said it was merely child's play, but Nāmaka knew better. The two sisters stared at each other with an intense dislike until the moment was broken by Hi'iaka, Pele's favorite sister.

Hi'iaka was the youngest and most loved of Pele's family and would soon join Pele on her journey. Hi'iaka was born in a special way, in the form of an egg, and was nurtured by Pele until she became a goddess. Together, the two formed a deep, loving friendship and sisterhood.

One day, Nāmaka returned from her travels through the waters of nearby islands. When she arrived home, she found much of the

---

2. This story by Linda Ching is adapted here with her permission from the following source: Linda Ching, *Hawaiian Goddesses*, Chapter 1. Honolulu, HI: Hawaiian Goddesses Publishing, 1987.

land burned and scalded by Pele's fiery work. Because of Pele's unquenchable desire and formidable power to change the land, Nāmaka convinced their mother, Haumea, that Pele should be banished. Haumea, earth mother and guardian of the sacred homeland, listened closely to Nāmaka. Finally, her heart heavy with sorrow, she decided that Nāmaka was right, that Pele must find a new place to work her powerful magic, one that would not destroy their home or *ohana* (family).

Pele did not fight against her dear mother's wishes. She took only two things with her: her magic firestick, which enabled her to connect with the inner fire of the land, and her beloved sister Hi'iaka. Other loyal attendants joined them, including several brothers and sisters who decided they wanted to live with Pele once she found a suitable place to reside. The group left their homeland in a sacred canoe and followed the stars across the Pacific.

Finally Pele reached the chain of Hawai'ian islands. But the first island in the chain was still too close to the water and Nāmaka's wrath. Similarly, her fire was too close to the water on the island of O'ahu. She moved on to Maui, leaving behind a trail of smoke and volcanic glow that rose up from the craters. This infuriated Nāmaka, who set out to destroy Pele once and for all. Before they fought, Pele made a deal with Nāmaka, that they would fight on their own terms, using their personal powers.

The destructive, wrathful fires of Pele rose up to meet the powerful waves of Nāmaka. They fought an entire day, masses of steam rising up between the wall of water and fountain of fire. Finally, Nāmaka, in her weariness, dishonored the fight and called Haui, the sea serpent, to her. Reinforced by his strength, Nāmaka and Haui defeated Pele and tore her body apart, scattering her bones on the island of Maui. Nāmaka gloated to the others of her victory for a short time, before one of the gods, Kāne, pointed to the sky above Hawai'i. There, over Mauna Loa and Mauna Kea, the mountains of

Hawai'i, the heavens were ablaze as if they had been set on fire. The spirit of Pele glowed in the skies, reborn in the ethers.

Pele again assumed human form and reunited with her family. They sailed to Hawai'i, the last island on the chain. As she climbed upon the new land, she felt a shudder of beauty and feeling of home move through her. She climbed up Kilauea and struck the earth a final time with her firestick. At that moment, she heard the 'elepaio bird sing and felt it was a favorable omen. She laughed with delight as she realized the site was perfect, far enough away from the wrath of Nāmaka. Pele worked with her stick, forming the crater and filling it with the boiling, molten lava and joyfully sending it down the slope into the sea. The work of the Fire Bearer could finally flourish. There, at the pit of Halema'uma'u, Pele took up residence with her family. She can be seen there to this day, still happily sending fiery lava destroying and creating land as is her wondrous passion. Pele brought her power of fire to the islands, a gift that reminds of continuous creation and destruction and inspires us to seek our own Fire Bearer within.

Keys to the Tale

Pele is different from her family; she has flaming red hair and is constantly drawn to fire. She is given the power of the firestick and uses it to draw up the fire of the earth, the intense power that is simultaneously creative and destructive, thus the archetype of the Fire Bearer. The importance of destruction, the "land eater" as Pele is called, is a clear reminder of this power. This links the Fire Bearer to the Crone, illuminating the cycles of birth, life, and death. Everywhere one drives around the island of Hawai'i, massive lava flows cross the landscape. Some are only a few decades old, a severe and poignant sign that life is impermanent and fragile. Pele's work reminds us that sometimes we need to destroy our habits, our tendencies, or dreams that are no longer working for us. Pele as Fire

Bearer teaches us to live fully, and consistently full of passion and clarity.

As the Fire Bearer, Pele symbolizes our inner, creative, wild fire. Many women feel a strong connection to her when they come to the island of Hawai'i. Her image of passionate beauty and fiery nature capture our hearts and we find ourselves dreaming of her, giving her offerings, and wanting to know her more intimately. She is the woman who would run with the wolves, so to speak, the wild woman as described by Clarissa Pinkola Estés, mythologist and researcher of the sacred feminine, the woman who is "…the Life/Death/Life force, she is the incubator. She is intuition, she is far-seer, she is deep listener, she is loyal heart. She encourages humans to remain multilingual; fluent in languages of dreams, passion, and poetry…These fill women with longing to find her, free her, and love her."[3] Pele cannot be contained or restrained, bearing her incredible power of the fire or digging stick and filled with unbridled passion. When we start the journey of the sacred feminine, we are inspired by Pele's gift of fire, using that to ignite our own spirit into creative action on the path.

Conversely, Nāmaka is the aspect of us that seeks to subdue our creativity, to limit our fearless and passionate self. She is the watery darkness or shadow side that threatens to put out our light, deny our magic, and cast us onto desolate shores. This aspect of our shadow wants to dampen our flame, just when it is beginning to glow, to take on fuel and expand. The shadow part that is not empowered seeks to destroy us before we can ever make progress. Our shadow aspect may be a result of trauma, programming from our family, religion, or society that tells us we cannot burn brightly, cannot access our authentic self; it is the small, persistent voice that says we are not worthy, we were born of sin, and there we will stay. We may feel the need to be validated by friends, boyfriends, or lovers to

---

3.   Clarissa Pinkola Estés, *Women Who Run with the Wolves*, p. 11.

deem ourselves worthy. Our negative inner voice may play a kind of tape that says things like, "He never responded to your message and thus you are not attractive or worthy of love." Yet, we *are* love—we are the Fire Bearer in potential. The desire for external acceptance is our inner Fire Bearer calling out to us to cultivate a powerful self-love that no longer needs the validation from others.

Nāmaka persuades their mother that Pele is too wild and head-strong for their homeland, that she will burn and destroy them with her fire. How many of us have similarly experienced this? Perhaps we too have been told that we are too fiery, destructive, and creative for our own good, and we must relegate ourselves to being the good girl, the obedient daughter, the noble follower. This serves to remind us our power needs an appropriate outlet. Part of the Fire Bearer's lesson is learning how, when, and where to channel our energies. Certain people, communities, or methods may not be the appro-priate place; we need to be surrounded by the *ohana* or family that nourishes our talents and does not fear us as Nāmaka fears Pele.

When we receive the touch of the Fire Bearer we must learn to manifest our rising power, creativity, while keeping our temper, anger, and wrath in balance. This is the shadow side of the Fire Bearer. Indeed, as in Pele's world, there is much to be angry about: the state of the world, the oppression of women still today, the burn-ing of witches and all the lost arts and medicines and wisdom. Yet, when we act from a place of anger and irrationality—when we react, rather than respond—we only generate more anger, more violence, more fuel for the destructive fires. That doesn't mean we should roll over and play dead when we hear of these problems, but we can cer-tainly use this anger in ways that are creative and powerful, just as Pele finds a place to create her art of birthing new land.

Pele's fiery nature is anchored by her dearest sister, Hi'iaka. Hi'iaka represents the pure heart of our being, the central aspect of ourselves that melts into love and beauty even amidst the powerful currents of emotion and chaos. She is the necessary love and compassion that aids our power as we walk the sacred feminine path. Cultivating a dear friendship with another woman helps immensely when we are working with power and transformation.

Similarly, it is also important to re-examine not only what works for us in terms of love relationships and careers, but also friendships. Surrounding ourselves with nourishing women who support our wild creative self is potent medicine for our own growth. On the other hand, if we have friends who mean well, but for some reason still cannot accept who we are, they may unintentionally act in ways that destroy our creative spirit, just as Nāmaka does toward Pele. Power-filled women realize that we cannot make all people happy or please everyone. Instead, we must make choices that honor our own real nourishment and our creative self; these choices do not always aid in soothing others' fears nor do they support dramas that drain us. Having a friend like Hi'iaka, one who clearly sees us through our own passions and vulnerability, enhances our powerful growth.

Pele finally faces Nāmaka in a duel where she is violently ripped to pieces by her sister and the sea serpent. The powerful act of dismemberment is found in cultural myths worldwide. Dionysus was torn to pieces by the Titans and his heart is taken by Athena, the goddess of wisdom, who gives him the gift of eternal knowledge. In the Vajrayana practice of Chöd in Tibetan Buddhism, the practitioner sacrifices her body to the hungry demons, part by part, through careful visualization. In this way, the ego is reduced, and true compassion and enlightenment can be achieved. This is a potent message of the Fire Bearer: that we must give up the smaller parts of ourselves in order to live from a place of power. This may mean the sacrifice of one's home or body as with Pele, or other things such as family, societal values, even friendships to align ourselves more deeply with spirit.

On my very first drum journey to the upper realms, I went through the process of dismemberment when I met the Tibetan

Red Tara. She had giant, ferocious, silvery teeth that I kept trying to imagine away, but as anyone who has done journey work knows, you cannot simply re-imagine your experience. Her teeth refused to disappear—on the contrary, she tore me apart, devoured me, and I was reborn into darkness. She took me to a narrow and precarious bridge that lay across an inestimably deep canyon and pointed to the bridge. "You have a long way to go," she smiled as I looked across the canyon uncertainly. This was a gift of the Fire Bearer and her wisdom, showing me that although I have learned a great deal, I still have a ways to go!

Pele is reborn in the sky, like the phoenix rising out of the ashes, coming into her full power as the Fire Bearer. Eventually, dismemberment leads to wholeness, re-membering, a unification of the lost pieces of oneself to form a newer, brighter, and more powerful self. Pele transforms into a human being and finally finds her home, her place to rest, create, and destroy at will. She is joined by her *ohana* and claims her home in the Halema'uma'u crater on Kilauea where she is still revered to this day. We too must learn how to re-member ourselves and reclaim our power. Starting with the ceremony below and continuing with the Initiate chapter, it is possible to heal ourselves of our own dismemberment and regain the powerful spirit that glows within.

EXERCISE 1.2

Forming a Women's Circle

Just as Pele forms a friendship with Hi'iaka and a tight circle of friends and family, you can also create a circle of close friends that support you on your path. This is crucial to your development as a woman who knows how to hold and work with power. It helps heal issues we hold in our role as a woman. So much of the time, judgment, comparison, gossip, and slander work between women to break up friendships and bonds. Jealousy is fierce among women in India, as a way to feel powerful in an otherwise disempowering situation. Coming together in circles of women, whether a one-time meeting or a closed group of the same women over the course of several years, supports work on our selves. Although much has changed and is changing among women, many of us still identify our power with qualities of a dominator system, a competitive way of looking at the world. This can be useful at times, but when we need to transform, to heal the abuse that was inflicted upon us, to nurture our intuition and our artistic selves, we need the support of other women who understand those specific issues and can help us define and dissolve them. Competing is not useful here, yet this is still a quest for power, a kind of power that is unique to us as women. Luckily, because we have come from a specific kind of system that has held sway for so long, we have the opportunity to be on the cutting edge of redefining power and reclaiming it for our own. Calling together women with whom we can connect and see through the ups and downs of having lovers and weddings, giving birth to babies and projects, sharing recipes and new ways to use software is also a very healing way to transform, grow, and let in more light.

Forming a women's circle can be as simple as getting together with women friends once a month. You may want to choose your meeting based on the moon cycles, meeting every new or full moon, and integrate ceremony and exercises from this book as part of your meeting. Meeting more often can be more powerful. These kinds of circles can be spontaneous as well and open to any women (and children too) who are interested in connecting with other women.

You may also choose to form a closed group where a set group of women meet over a period of time. It is helpful to have a vision for the group from the beginning to give it some direction. For example, you may want to name the group and decide on specific things you want to do, such as (but not limited to): full or new moon ceremony; initiation work, ceremony, and exercises like the ones found in upcoming chapters of this book; storytelling, music, art, and/or dance creations; community service projects that could include anything from donating clothes to offering performances at the local community center. Having a specific purpose or function helps to focus the group initially although your focus may change over time. After a year or so, you may choose to open the circle up again to get fresh people and ideas into the group, or you may leave it closed for several years and perhaps host open circles at times for various purposes.

Suggested Women's Circle Format

When forming a women's circle, you will need to choose where you will meet. You may choose to rotate between each other's homes or one set place, such as one home or a yoga studio, which can often be rented for a reasonable rate. You will want to set how often you meet and whether the circle is open or closed. Before each circle (or at the end of a meeting), decide what you will be focusing on, such as a new moon ceremony, initiation process, or healing work. You may want to bring offerings for the altar, food for afterward, a monetary donation if you are renting a space, and anything else appropriate for your circle. Other items may include drums, mats to lie on, ritual objects, or oracles (such as tarot cards or runes). Usually the facilitator is also the main space holder for each circle, but if it is a set place, then this can rotate or change as needed. Below are suggested steps for a meeting:

- **Smudge or purification:** As each woman enters the home or space, have a designated woman (the facilitator or first arrival) purify or cleanse her. You can use various ways to purify, such as a feather, a brush, a traditional smoking herb such as sage, ringing chimes, or using an anointing oil. This allows each woman to be honored upon arriving and lets her soul check into shifting from mundane daily drama and plans into the nurturing and intuitive space of a women's circle.

- **Mingling and connecting:** Before sitting down in the circle, women love to chat and reconnect from their last meeting. Allow some time for this, to integrate into the group once again. If it is an open group, new arrivals like the chance to open up in smaller groups before forming the main circle.

- **Brief check-in:** Once everyone has arrived, sit in a circle and go around announcing names and making brief introductions as needed. This is also a time to mention what you are going through, as pertaining to the circle. This should be somewhat brief; if needed, the facilitator may gently encourage the circle to continue. It is nice to use a talking stick (or rattle, etc.) to pass around and hold while talking. This helps to limit interruptions and gives each person a chance to share.

- **Ceremonial work:** The facilitator for the evening should then introduce whatever kind of work the group has chosen for the evening. If it is a ceremony, she, along with other group members, may have organized different roles for different members of the circle to participate in. This may be a time to do healing work, initiations, or create music and/or art. There are several ceremonies in this book that can be used as models for various women's circle meetings. Also see "Creating your Own Ceremony" in Chapter Eight for further tips. If the circle is working toward a particular goal, such as creating a fundraiser for a local community center, then this is the time for generating ideas, creating projects as needed, and setting goals.

- **Closing the circle:** Once you have finished your core work for the evening, take time to close and feel gratitude for coming together. You are still in sacred space at this time, and it is important to connect back in on that deep level before dispersing, mingling, and eating. This is also a time to share anything in the group, such as a healing experience that happened during the meeting. It can also be a time to decide when the next meeting will be, the location, and the focus.

- **Sharing and integrating:** After the circle has been formally closed, there should be enough time to share food and continue to connect as needed. This helps to integrate and ground whatever has been experienced during the circle and reconnect with friends before parting ways.

New Moon Ceremony: Creating Fertile Ground

The Fire Bearer speaks to us of new beginnings, creativity, and rebirth out of destruction. The seed or ember of our inner fire can be revisited each month or season to clear away what is no longer needed and empower our creative ventures. Creating a new moon ceremony is a perfect opportunity to revisit our inner fire and release the old. The new moon is the time when no moon is visible in the sky. This is a ritual for going within and opening yourself up for transformation as well as seeding new ideas, plans, or projects. This will give you the opportunity to discover what fulfills you and create it more fully in your life. This ceremony can be done alone or with others. If you choose to do it with others, be sure to choose women whom you can entrust your deep feelings with, as you will be releasing doubts and fears in this ceremony.

Gather together the following items:

- Offerings for the four or six directions (see "Creating Sacred Space" in the Introduction)
- Pictures and images that speak to you about transformation and creating a ground that will prepare you for newness, such as a dark circle or image of the new moon, or a picture of something emerging from the ground
- A picture of Pele from the myth

- Music and rhythm makers
- Six candles for the four directions, mother earth (below), and father sky (above), and one black candle
- A foot bath with warm water
- A soothing oil such as lavender or rose
- Paper and pen
- A cauldron or small pot to burn things in
- A separate smaller bowl of water
- Several seeds of one or more plants or flowers
- A small cloth pouch
- A tarot deck or other oracle if you use them

Dress in clothing that feels like rebirth; black is appropriate as the color of the void and the womb, but anything that speaks to you of transformation is fine. You can think of the dark soil which seeds are planted in. Although plants eventually need the brilliance of the sun, seeds are in darkness before sprouting, just as we are in the womb before birth. If you bleed on the new moon, consider offering a bit of collected blood to the earth during this ceremony or at least not wearing a tampon. Allow yourself to really feel the pulse of your womb as you create ceremony, as women have done for thousands of years.

Create your altar in a place that will not be disturbed. Use a black or deep indigo cloth to cover a small table to indicate the ground of death and dark soil. Set up your images and any other offerings such as flowers, incense, stones, feathers, and crystals. Place a candle in each of the four directions, either on the perimeter of your circle or directly on your altar; place the mother earth and father sky candles on the altar as well as the black candle, paper and pen, cloth pouch, and oracle. Sit or lie quietly in a meditative space for several minutes, to relax your mind and quiet your body.

When you are ready, cast a circle or create sacred space. Call in each of the directions, east, south, west, and north, and their respective elements: air, fire, water, and earth. As you call them in using your voice, drum, or other sound maker, try to really feel the element moving through you and into your circle. If you have a group of people, different women may call the directions. Once you call them in, give the appropriate offerings for each, such as incense for the east, lava rock or fire for the south, water for the west, and salt for the north. Then light the candle in the appropriate direction. Next, call mother earth. You can use any name that you associate with the earth. Thank her for her gifts; make sure to feel a strong sense of gratitude here—you are a part of her, as living flesh and blood. Light a candle to honor the mother earth. Then call in father sky, or simply the star, moon, and sun qualities. I often link the starlight to my ancestors; when we look upon the stars we are looking into the past. Light a candle for father sky. Finally, call in the center and feel the power of your being that connects the six directions, uniting in the center. Visualize yourself as the central point between the four cardinal directions. Then imagine yourself as a channel between earth and sky, holding your arms up toward the stars, feeling the earth under your feet. Know that you are a pulsing, breathing, living being full of spirit and power, just like the earth and all that is around you. Visualize your sacred space as a flaming circle surrounding you, protecting you and illuminating your space that is now between the worlds.[4]

Once you have filled your circle with energy, lie back and enjoy the glow. If you are working with guides, take a few moments to call in your guides, ancestors, or any spirit beings that you feel connected to. Next, wash your feet with the foot basin, symbolizing

---

4. Use your sound makers, drums, and voice to raise the energy in the circle. Dancing and singing are also a good way to bring up power and fill you with energy for performing the ceremony.

purification. If you are doing the ceremony in a group, have one or two women wash the feet of the circle members, followed by anointing the feet with oil. This symbolizes washing away doubt and fear, opening up to what will follow. This is also a moment of trust, allowing another woman to wash our feet and be gentle and nurturing with us. (Make sure they get their turn too.)

Then invoke the power of the Fire Bearer either as an archetype or specifically as Pele. If you do not connect with the idea of a goddess, simply light your black candle and invoke the power of rebirth. It is important to do this aloud, to use your voice and sound makers to call in this energy, to really allow yourself to communicate that to the deeper aspects of your subconscious.

Next, take some time to write down things you want to clear, such as fears, obstacles, or doubts. Make a list, being very clear what it is you are attempting to clear. Some good examples are: my fear that I do not have enough; my fear of death and dying; my depression; my anger; my ill health. You are using the power of the Fire Bearer here, really calling in the energy of destroying to make room for the new. This is not necessarily going to happen in one ritual, but it is an important first step to allow those doubts and fears to surface so that you may begin the process of shedding and transforming. I strongly encourage that you then call these issues out into the night, so that they may be heard and borne away with the guidance of your ancestors and helpers. After you call them out, light the paper on fire in the black candle and let it burn in the bowl or cauldron. Watch as the fire takes your paper and symbolically turns it to ash, something to give back to the earth. Use the ashes to fertilize a favorite plant or tree. You can also mix some of your moon blood with the ashes.

Once you have completed the clearing away part of the ritual, then pour some of the clean, fresh water from the smaller bowl over your head or splash it in your face. This is to symbolize that the clearing has begun. If you do the ritual with others, you may want to

have them close their eyes, then circle around and splash them, sur-
prising them into a new state of consciousness. It is amazing what a
simple splash in the face can do to open up our minds!

Now is the time to decide something you want to do or create in
your life in the next month. This can be small or big, something you
have wanted to do that you haven't allowed yourself time for such
as starting a garden, doing a work of art, going to visit a place you
are interested in. Pass out seeds to the others, or take them yourself and make an intention for your coming days ahead. I prefer to
make only one or two very clear intentions, so as not to scatter this
potent energy into too many whims and wishes. Some examples of
intentions are: I am clear and happy and bright; I am abundant and
flowing with money; I am becoming a more loving person; I intend
to travel to South America. Blow your intention into the seeds and
then keep them for symbolic planting by placing them on your altar
or in the small pouch.

If you choose to, you can now take some time to work with an
oracle. This is useful for guidance on the next phase of your life, be
it the next month or year, or specific guidance for a coming change,
the transformation you are undergoing, on a particular project or
new idea. For this I will usually separate my tarot deck, using just
the Major Arcana, and choose one card as guidance for the coming
days. Sometimes I use my goddess oracle cards, again just choosing
one and letting that single symbol speak to me. I find it is important
in magical work to keep certain things simple, rather than pulling
too many cards to try to get what we want. Otherwise the energy
can dissolve and the magic disintegrates as our need to control and
rationalize takes over.

The final aspect of the ritual is the closing. Make sure your
seeds are securely put away on the altar or in your pouch and also
carefully put away the tarot deck or other oracle. Leave the black
candle to burn down through the night, carrying your releases
onward, if it is safe to do so. (If you cannot leave the candle burning,

then put it out with a candle snuffer.) Thank the center, father sky, and mother earth, followed by the directions, going counterclockwise: north, west, south, east. As you thank each direction, snuff out the candle with wet fingers or a snuffer, allowing the direction and its element to "Go if you must, stay if you will." Visualize the circle dissolving, the directions merging back into all that is. Take a few moments to sit quietly and think of all the amazing things in your life, right here and now, that you have to be grateful for. Leave the ashes and the seeds on the altar until morning, or you may put the seeds under your pillow to encourage sacred dreams; throw the footbath water out into the garden.

two

The Initiate
Reclaiming the Dark Mother

One thing that comes out in myths
is that at the bottom of the abyss comes the voice
of salvation. The black moment is the moment
when the real message of transformation is going to
come. At the darkest moment comes the light.
—Joseph Campbell

Imagine you are on the lip of a canyon, looking out across
a deep rift in the earth. Within the canyon, dark and wild
below, is an inky black crack in the earth that holds no light.
On the other side of the canyon is a meadow filled with
beautiful trees, and instantly you know that place; it is your
inner garden, your own secret place of nourishment and joy.
As you glance below, wondering how you will cross over to
the other side, the wind suddenly picks up, blowing across
your face and whipping your hair around. The breeze feels
good and alive, calling you to your sacred garden that awaits
you. Yet, you know that to get there, you must first descend

into the darkness below, to become the Initiate. There is no other way to reach the garden that awaits you. In your mind's eye, you see the dark cave deep in the earth; it is frightening, but it is also filled with glittering, golden boxes that overflow with treasure. Outside the cave is a fierce dragon, a monster that bares its teeth, illuminating your inner fear. Yet you carry the torch of the Fire Bearer and you call out for guidance as you begin to make your way into the unknown below. You feel the reassuring presence of a guide next to you, supporting your descent. In your mind, worries dissolve and you know that by facing the darkness below, you will re-emerge as the power-filled Initiate.

We have planted our Fire Bearer seeds and are ready to cross the threshold into an even more power-filled place on the sacred feminine journey: the path of the Initiate. The Initiate is the part of us that is willing to face our inner darkness within and transform pain and fear into power. This often requires a leap of faith, an initiation into the mysteries of the sacred feminine. In this chapter, the Initiate comes in the form of Inanna, the ancient Sumerian goddess who descended deep into the underworld to face the dark mother and after three days was reborn anew. This chapter contains several exercises along with the myth and ceremony to work with meeting your inner Initiate.

Initiation is a deep surrender; it is the courage to really give ourselves over to the universe, goddess, or larger self. When we are initiated, we are taking the great leap into the unknown; it is a complete letting go. Giving birth is an example of initiation where we must completely let go, in a way that is also active, wild, and has the potential to be deeply empowering. Other forms of initiation include times when we have faced inner turmoil, deep loss, or a vast mystery. Can you remember a time in the night when you cried so hard in your desperate fear of losing control that indeed a shift occurred? This is a form of initiation.

The Initiate's path into power enables us to meet the dark mother who lives in the recesses of our being. The dark mother comes in several mythic forms throughout history. Goddesses of ancient times abound in guarding the underworld, a place of rest for the dead or associated with the ocean of blood, the primordial life force of the universe and earth. Ereshkigal (who is featured in the myth below) is the dark mother visited by Inanna. Kali, the black, fearsome Hindu goddess, slays illusion with her curved sword; Hecate is a Greek dark goddess of death and magic; Hel is the Norse queen of the underworld; and Lilith, whose name means night, was considered Adam's first wife. Lilith refused to lay under him or submit to his dominance and was later demonized into a harlot of hell by overzealous religiosity. This fall from grace and power is a lesson in the story of the dark mother, who has been pushed underground for the last several thousand years. Many goddesses were demolished, demonized, demoted, or completely changed from powerful female forms into male rulers and gods.

The dark mother is one of the fiercest aspects of the goddess; she is the wild and untamable part of our selves. Here we find rage, fury, sorrow, fear, pain, guilt, and despair as well as limitlessness, depth, ancientness, the wilderness, and portals into the unknown. Much of the power of the dark goddess has been relegated to what we associate with negative, bad, even evil. As the ancient worship of the sacred feminine shifted into predominate masculine power, we find that not only goddesses but all things female become relegated to this terrible, sinful state. In several cultures, women, birth, indigenous people, dark forests, menstruation, blood, sickness, old age, and death all became associated with evil, the devil, and sinister devouring. These qualities may surface as we face our inner self, confront her, and finally surrender to the shadow aspects that are not allowing us to grow more firmly into power. The feminine qualities of darkness, moistness, birth, and blood symbolize the dark mother and our inner Initiate. We have been taught to deny these parts of our selves and bodies; honoring the sacred feminine invites you to reclaim these as not only part of who you are, but a powerful aspect of your life.

When we face our shadow, we are initiated into our deepest powers. We may be afraid of these parts; these howling, undernourished, repressed, and rage-filled aspects of ourselves that demand to be heard, but which we cannot bear to face. Perhaps we are comfortable in our denial or deadened enough to simply tread water, keeping our head up, looking toward the brilliant sky and sun without realizing the murky water is damaging to our being and needs to be made clear.

When I was nineteen I had cancer, a life-changing and initiatory event. The journey into fear and illness, through and back into regular life, had the hallmarks of initiation. I had to give up things, face my fears, choose to live, then navigate back to wellness, shedding the symbolic skins (my hair falling out) and finding a source of joy and inspiration (dance, art, and school). The journey was not easy, but what made it bearable were my family and my dance community.

There are two ways to confront the lost parts of our selves and reclaim our feminine power: willingly and unwillingly. I have both willingly and unwillingly been initiated into the dark parts of my self. I have brought back many gifts, yet there were many long months of pain and depression before I surfaced. Unwillingly I dealt with cancer at nineteen. When I was twenty-six, my first-born daughter died just a few days after birth. Both of those experiences forced me to face dark parts of myself. Willingly I have worked on deep healing of my own trauma around these instances, healing my wounds. At some point it becomes necessary to face the darkness and embrace it. We can recognize that moving through darkness is an initiation into power. Once this happens, we no longer need to continue identifying so strongly with suffering and our personal drama; we become strong and full of power.

Whether we decide to deliberately enter the darkness or have been cast there unwillingly, the Initiate asks us to journey into the unknown. This is where guidance becomes essential to our development. We may choose to ask for female guidance, such as the dark mother, Mary or Green Tara, our own mother or grandmother, or our own higher self. If you are accustomed to calling on the god as your guidance, I encourage you to open up to the feminine aspect of the divine. Call her "the mother" if "the goddess" feels too difficult. Try, because you are in a female form.

Ancestral Gifts

The first step in empowering our inner Initiate is to ask for help. In our current society of fierce independence and value on self-advancement, this is an important step in surrendering to the larger connection of our world and universe and aids in activation of the Initiate. When you read Inanna's myth below, you'll see that her helper, her sister Ninshubur, was crucial in aiding her return from the underworld. Similarly, Hi'iaka, a kind sister, supported Pele in her times of darkness as Fire Bearer. Traditional cultures use ancestors and spirit guides to help during major life changes, receiving healing, and answering bigger life questions. If you have never used guides, this is a perfect time to begin working with them. There are several types of guides we can connect with, and we will work with different ones at different points in this book.

Our first personal guide connection is to our ancestors. Our DNA carries the imprints of our genealogical lineage and has a direct influence on our lives. We are intricately connected to the people in our families, who deeply influence our lives whether we realize it or not. An immediate connection to our sacred feminine lies in the stories of our grandmothers, our mothers, and our aunts.

Not only are they our relatives, they are also the first glimpses of feminine power that entered our consciousness as small children. By connecting with our female ancestors, we have the opportunity to honor their gifts as well as heal the pain they may have suffered while on earth.

I have a strong, spiritual connection with my Hungarian grandmother. When she was alive, I could often feel her pain or joy from hundreds of miles away, and she would know when I was visiting my parents' home, calling on the phone to speak with me. I inherited her sharp, penetrating mind and clear vision. My other grandmother, my mother's mother, took up quilting late in her life. Her beautiful stitching and creative combinations surrounded me as a child along with the homemade dresses she crafted for my sister and me. She was also a brilliant letter writer, describing family events through letters to people throughout her life. I feel I've inherited her gifts as weaver and storyteller. I also connect with my daughter who died a few days after birth, Rubybleu. Very soon after her death, I was overwhelmed by the sense that she had become my ancestor. Although I am her mother and I gave birth to her, her spirit is a guide, a relative connected by blood who has crossed over. The experience of losing Rubybleu left me with many gifts. One of those gifts is my growing capacity to sense and communicate with unborn baby spirits around women and families. Honoring the ancestors nourishes us and is a potent guide for working with initiation on the sacred feminine path.

EXERCISE 2.1

Calling on Guidance and the Ancestors

Connecting with our feminine ancestors and sending healing is a potent way to reclaim our power as women. Sometimes we are given very clear messages about how we can further honor our ancestors and may feel compelled to research their stories, do a DNA test to find out our ancestry (especially descendants of slaves, who often have broken family trees), or collect letters and photographs from the past. This helps give a voice to the stories that are flowing through our blood, connects us to the larger family tree, and helps us see how diverse and interconnected we are.

Spend time at your altar that you constructed in the exercise in the Introduction. Continue to add images of the sacred feminine, of goddesses; photos and jewelry from your mother, grandmothers, aunts; symbols that represent the divine feminine, such as circles, snakes, images of the moon, the yoni, and plants. Create sacred space by calling in the directions and casting a circle. Then sit quietly and think of your feminine ancestors. Light candles in their honor if you wish. First thank them for their gifts, stories, and joys that they shared with you. Think of all the things they did in their lifetimes: the meals they cooked, the children they raised, the gardens they tended, the people they loved. Think back over the stories of their lives and open your heart in gratitude and connection. Know that in your bones is the DNA that you have inherited from them and that the stories from woman to woman have inevitably been passed down to you. Give an offering on your altar in memory of these women, perhaps flowers, beads, or something that reminds you of them. If you have jewelry from your grandmothers or mother, choose to wear it for one moon (one month) to relate to their power, calling in their wisdom and connecting to your family's sacred feminine.

As you sit in the candlelight, you may also want to ask for specific guidance from your grandmother (I use the word "grandmother," but this could be any female deceased relative). Concentrate on the breath and the intention to connect with your feminine ancestors. Imagine one of your grandmothers sitting across from you. She is sending you love and light, and you can send love and light back to her. Feel the exchange between the two of you and spend several moments honoring the healing energy. When you feel ready, form a question clearly in your mind. Ask your question either silently or aloud and visualize her receiving the question. Sit quietly for some time and wait for a response.

You may also ask questions using the journey method (see the second part of Exercise 2.2 on page 41) or an oracle such as tarot cards. You may experience a symbolic answer. Make sure to write down the cards or messages you receive and leave them to analyze later. When you feel your grandmother has answered, wait a few more moments and see if you need to ask anything else, either for clarification or a further question. Again, wait and receive the message, writing it down. You may want to also ask her if there is anything you should do to help maintain your connection with your ancestors. Once I was told by a psychic to eat cabbage to work with my ancestors. Well, my grandmother was Hungarian and cabbage is a very common food in Hungary! It seemed silly at first, but not only have I eaten cabbage since then, I have learned some of the dishes my grandmother used to make and feel I am honoring her each time I cook them.

When you are finished, send healing love and golden light to your grandmother. Take some time to generate gratitude in your heart for connecting with her. Imagine her surrounded by a golden bubble and floating off and away into the universe. She is moving on for now, but you know in your heart that you can access her as needed.

After you have comfortably accessed your matrilineal side, try connecting with your grandfathers, fathers, and uncles in the same way. Feel the wisdom from the male side of your family that also flows through your blood, the adventure, courage, strength, and visionary aspects of the men who have seeded the women in your family. This promotes healing for men in your family who have also suffered suppression in the past. When you have completed your efforts, again thank the ancestors. Close the sacred space and honor each of the elements.

When you go to sleep, set an intention to dream of your ancestors. Be open to the messages and omens that may appear in the days that follow. When I began working on this book, I began to have more dreams of my Hungarian grandmother in particular. One dream was especially powerful, as she visited me in glowing light and stressed that she was not dead, but alive and well. She looked radiant and beautiful, sitting atop her hospital bed, and I was filled with joy at seeing her again. When I woke up, I looked at the calendar and realized it was April 23, the anniversary of my *other* grandmother's passing! The two were inextricably linked in my own mind from that point on and I use their guidance as needed.

Inanna

Inanna is the Sumerian name for the goddess who is queen of all the heavens and earth. She is the mother of culture, the great goddess of the Fertile Crescent who ruled over the abundant lands of Sumer, today known as Iraq. As history unfolded, Inanna transformed into Ishtar, Astarte, and later Athena and Aphrodite. Inanna bestowed upon humans the gifts of civilization, called the *me* or mother-wisdom, including arts such as writing, literature, law, calendars, and engineering. Grain was sacred to Inanna, and the connection between food, growth, and women and their monthly cycles was honored by ancient people of Sumer.

One of the oldest stories on earth is the myth of Inanna's descent into the underworld. This tale of sacrifice, death, and rebirth is far older than the story of Christ, although we can find similarities in their stories. Inanna's descent was written on clay tablets sometime around 1750 BCE, although many historians believe the myth is much older than that and was passed down orally for thousands of years prior to its inscription.

Inanna's descent is told in many books on the sacred feminine and the goddess and in connection with initiation. Why do women keep returning to this story to understand ourselves? What is it about delving into the depths of darkness? Why might we feel compelled to suddenly start visiting caves—or give up on our career and take to gardening or drumming or dreaming? In Estés's words, "*La selva subterranea*, the underground forest, the underworld of female knowing…is a wild world that lives under this one, under the world perceived by ego. While there, we are infused with instinctive language and knowledge. From that vantage point we understand what cannot be so easily understood from the point of view of the topside world."[5] When we consciously decide to go to the underworld, sacrificing the outer aspects of our little self, we meet the shadow of our larger self, reclaim her and bring her back, empowered. Working to reclaim the shadow helps to accept ourselves exactly as we are, then transform the shadow from fear into power. Inanna's story shows us there is a way out, and although it is difficult, it is essential to our wholeness as women.

The Descent of Inanna

Inanna, the great Queen of Heaven and Earth, felt a strange desire growing in her heart. She yearned to visit the underworld, a place that no man or woman ever visits before their death. Yet Inanna wished to visit her sister, Ereshkigal, the Queen of the Underworld, who ruled the land of death, darkness, and decay, and to honor the recent death of Ereshkigal's husband.

Before proceeding, Inanna called on her dear sister and friend Ninshubur and carefully instructed her that if she had not returned from the underworld in three days, Ninshubur should mourn for her and beat the drum in all the places where people gather. Inanna also told her to visit each of the fathers of culture and ask them for help. Then Inanna paused, looked deeply in Ninshubur's eyes and said, "Now go, Ninshubur, but do not forget my words."

---

5.   Estés, p. 389.

Inanna prepared carefully for her journey. She dressed in beautiful robes and anointed herself with aromatic oils. She adorned herself with seven ornaments symbolizing the seven *me* or mother-powers of civilization. She placed a crown on her head, a shining golden pendant on her forehead, and took a rod of lapis lazuli in her hand. Small lapis lazuli stones she fastened around her neck and a double strand at her breast, with gold bracelets on her wrists and a golden breastplate.

Then she crossed over the great plains and arrived at the gates of the underworld. There, at the first gate, Inanna stopped and declared herself to Neti, the gatekeeper. Neti announced Inanna's arrival to Ereshkigal, the Queen of the Underworld. Ereshkigal writhed in her fury at Inanna's boldness. She told Neti, "Inanna may enter only if she is naked and bowed low to the ground!"

Inanna proceeded and Neti removed one of Inanna's seven ornaments at each of the seven gates and finally stripped her completely naked. Inanna arrived at Ereshkigal's underworld, naked and bowed low. The dark mother Ereshkigal sat upon her throne with the seven judges, the Annunaki, before Inanna as she bowed to them, her forehead grazing the hard ground. They fixed the stone-cold eyes of death upon Inanna, and in that moment, Inanna was turned into a corpse and hung from a hook on the wall.

For three days and three nights, Inanna hung rotting on the wall. When she did not return to the upper world, Ninshubur mourned for Inanna. As asked, she beat the drum in all the places where people gather and went to each of the fathers of culture to ask them for help. Ninshubur visited Enlil, the highest god of earth and sky, and Nanna-Sin, the god of the moon. Both flatly refused to help Inanna as they were not inclined to tread on Ereshkigal's territory. But father Enki, god of water and wisdom, accepted Ninshubur's plea for help and created two sexless spirits from under the dirt of his fingernail. He gave them the water and food of life and sent them to the underworld.

When they reached the underworld, the two spirits found Ereshkigal writhing in pain, in birth and in sorrow. The spirits mirrored Ereshkigal's moans with their own cries of pain and sorrow. Ereshkigal, moved by their sympathy, asked the two spirits what they wanted. They requested Inanna's life. After some deliberation, Ereshkigal brought Inanna down from her hook and laid her on the ground. The spirits gave Inanna the food and water of life and she opened her eyes.

Awakened from her three days of death, Inanna began her journey back to the upper world. But before she left, Ereshkigal reminded her that someone must take her place. No one can leave the underworld unaffected, and Ereshkigal sent her demons after Inanna. The demons scampered at her heels as she journeyed back to her home, reclaiming her clothing and ornaments at each of the seven gates.

Inanna returned to the world of humans as both victorious goddess and a woman plagued with demonic shadows. She embraced her dear Ninshubur with gratitude for her courage and support. Then Inanna knew she must find someone to take her place in the underworld. Upon her return, she found that her lover, Dumuzi, had been making plans to take over her rule during her absence. She was furious and sent him with the demons to take her place in the underworld. Every year Dumuzi must return to the underworld for six months. Even though it was her own fury that sent Dumuzi below, Inanna wept for his absence. To this day, during Inanna's time of sorrow, winter settles in on the realms of earth and sky each year.

Keys to the Tale

In this classic tale of initiation, Inanna descends to the underworld. She shows incredible courage and fearlessness, and consciously chooses to undertake a journey that may lead to her own death. At first glance, this may not seem common for many of us unless we are extreme adventure enthusiasts—few people willingly choose a journey that will end in certain death. Yet, we do things throughout our lives that are threatening or at least scary, such as giving birth, deciding to get divorced, or traveling to a new place.

Inanna asks Ninshubur to help her if she does not return after three days. Ninshubur is like the bridge between our conscious and subconscious selves. This is crucial in our initiatory process. Having a friend or guide act as a helper during our own initiatory reclaiming helps us to stay connected to the present and our conscious selves. Sometimes when we pull up old memories of buried trauma, it may unleash rage, fear, or sorrow. Having someone to help us anchor these feelings is important.

Inanna specifically instructs Ninshubur to beat the drum for her, an act that is akin to the work of a shaman. Shamans, like Inanna, journey to the underworld regularly to seek information or missing soul pieces for healing and divination. The drum is the most common way that shamans enter an altered state to conduct this journey. Layne Redmond, a woman drummer and explorer of the sacred feminine, notes that "drumming is the traditional means used by shamans to descend to the underworld and return. Often during a shamanic trance the shaman's assistant takes over the playing of the drum to maintain the link between the worlds. Without the sound of the drum to lead the way, the shaman would be lost forever in the underworld."[6] We can use drumming to aid us in journeying to the lower realms, as explored in Exercise 2.2.

As Inanna descends into the underworld, she must face seven gates. Neti, the gatekeeper, symbolizes the part of us that allows each of the roles and identities to be shed away. At each gate Inanna is asked to remove something from her body. Inanna's descent perhaps inspired the story of Salome in the Old Testament. Salome

---

6. Layne Redmond, *When the Drummers Were Women*, p. 87.

performs the dance of the seven veils for King Herod, removing each veil during her dance to send him into a lustful rage. The seven veils represent the seven layers of illusion or earthly appearances that fall away during the descent into the great mystery. The seven gates are also symbols for each of the chakras found in yogic philosophy, which hold the seeds of conscious awareness and are used for spiritual development. Symbolically, Inanna's removal of each item represents contact with each chakra or a different level of consciousness. Facing each gate symbolizes our own path of initiation in which we move through the obstacles of each level of consciousness before finally reaching the deepest parts of the subconscious.

Once Inanna is stripped down and completely naked, only then may she enter into the deepest part of herself. This is an essential aspect of initiation, the stripping down of our various selves, our ego, our attachments, and our desires. Real transformation cannot happen until we dissolve these qualities. In initiatory experiences, we are often forced to surrender roles. When I lost my first-born daughter, I was stripped of the role of mother. Although I had given birth, I suddenly had no child to raise and was forced to face the sorrow that followed. If we get divorced, we are stripped of the role of wife; if we lose the use of a part of our body, we are stripped of being a healthy, whole person. I have found that the more deeply we face the darkness that is really a form of initiation, the more power we receive and the less we suffer afterward.

Once Inanna has arrived in the underworld, she meets the cold eye of Ereshkigal. This eye symbolizes the quiet and solemn witness that resides within us who unerringly sees all sides of our situation. This is the part of us that enables us to somehow allow those old roles to die. In fact, sometimes there is a bit of strange joy in that moment; a glimpse of real freedom, a self undefined and beyond the constraints of hope or loss.

Inanna faces Ereshkigal, who is writhing in pain, in birth, defecating and bleeding. Ereshkigal is potent yet completely vulnerable, portraying the very real aspects of life: power and suffering all mixed up together and inseparable. When we come to face this reality, we are transformed and realize, on a deep level, there is nothing to fear and we are the source of our own pain as well as the creator of our inner fire and power. We can each recall a moment in our lives when we faced our fear, then suddenly saw it for what it was: nothing more than our own small mind projecting something scary. I remember being so frightened when I first found out I had cancer. I was in a dark place for about a week when suddenly I felt as if I could make a choice: live or die. I simply chose to live and my fear evaporated.

Inanna hangs on a hook underground for three days just as the moon is new over a three-day period. Traditionally, this time is associated with menstruation and is like a monthly initiation or small death in itself, when our body sheds the old blood, making room for the new. Vicki Noble explores this power, saying, "We just need to understand that *the monthly menstrual period is the quintessential ritual experience*, analogous to the time of the Dark Moon—the impossibly magical time when the moon disappears from the sky and then through a miraculous rebirth appears once more; and the impossibly magical time when women, without a wound, bleed from the sacred yoni for three days."[7] Culturally, we have been shut off from this powerful part of ourselves every month. We cycle, just as the moon cycles. This may seem unimportant, but it is as important as the tides of this earth: it has the potential to affect everything around us. Taking time to spend our moon days doing nourishing things for our body, mind, and spirit allows us to more deeply participate with a monthly initiation. If we pay close attention, we may find we are more psychic at this time and have more visions and powerful dreams. In the ceremony below, you have the

---

7. Vicki Noble, *Shakti Woman*, p. 95.

opportunity to reclaim your first menses, the incredible, sacred time of becoming a woman.

When Inanna does not return from the underworld, Ninshubur sets off to ask for help from the three fathers of culture. The first two fathers tell Ninshubur that Inanna does not deserve to return, that she must stay in the underworld. The fathers in the story symbolize the part of us that can help face our darkest fears. They are the logical, clear-sighted helpers who can create the necessary mirrors but do not have to become emotionally involved. In shamanic healing, we work to dissolve the patterns without necessarily having to express each and every emotion.

Enki fashions two beings, the genderless spirits, to assist Ninshubur in reclaiming Inanna from her three days in the underworld. Their gift is to deeply mirror the dark mother's loneliness and function as witnesses to Ereshkigal's massive pain. By watching her intimately and moaning with her, they are seeing her sorrow, her decay, her ferment, and Ereshkigal is deeply moved. This is an important aspect of the healing process. When a part of us or someone else witnesses our darkness, our pain, when we have guides to help us along the way, two things happen: first, the pain is lessened, and second, we realize how much we are responsible for our own suffering. This empowers us to really transform the pain into something useful—to drop the drama and heal the trauma. As a practicing Reiki master for over a decade, I have found that admitting our pain and telling someone else is the first step toward our empowerment.

In the final section of the story, Inanna arises and returns to her city. She is reborn after three days of death and decay, just as the moon reappears from the sky after three days. Like any good fairy tale, Inanna's rebirth does not come without a price. She is followed back up to the normal world, the world of the conscious mind, by the demons. Often when we pass through an initiatory experience such as illness, death of a loved one, or depression, the darkness does not leave us, but becomes a kind of lesson that stays with us. This knowing is profound; it enables us to more deeply understand human pain and suffering. The darkness can also be full of gifts such as connections to ancestors or spirits, healing powers, or simply a deeper compassion for suffering.

Reclaiming Our Initiation

The story of Inanna tells of a deliberate, willing descent into the underworld; it is the story of initiation and is an inspiration to aid us on our own journey to recover our darkness within. The power of the Initiate is truly transformative. By reclaiming our initiation, we will discover our inner powerful potential, cleanse out of our lives what no longer serves us, and open up the path to create a life that is imbued with joy. Our society does not have a specialized initiatory process, and so we must use our own past and reclaim our initiations. Looking back over our lives, we find specific events that have occurred which caused great change in our lives. Perhaps it was illness, an accident, the death of a loved one, divorce, or other trauma. We are first looking to find a significant event that caused some kind of pain or trauma which we then grew out of.

To reclaim is to reframe that event, to begin to dialogue about it in a new way. For example, I have a friend who was in a traumatic motorcycle accident several years ago. Whenever I ask her for some information that she cannot immediately recall, she blames it on the accident, saying it has destroyed her memory. This may be true. But it may also have done something to rewire her brain in a way that is beneficial. Perhaps her keen intuition, which is extremely accurate, was enhanced by her accident. I do not want to gloss over a trauma in someone's life, in a new-age manner of denial and "only thinking in the positive," but I do believe that we get in the habit of relegating "negative" aspects of ourselves to events that changed everything. When we do this, we may miss the inherent gifts that arise when we go through this initiatory event. By reclaiming the event, we can figure out why it is important to our life and relevant to the work we are doing on earth. At the very least, using the following exercises, we can drum up some gratitude for what has happened, looking at how it has happened and the fact that we survived. It's a bit cliché, but seriously, "What doesn't kill us, makes us stronger."

Another aspect of reclaiming initiation is to face a story and then dissolve it. This releases patterns we are holding on to and opens us up to receive incredible power. Just as stones or brambles get caught in the flow of a river, past traumas can stay caught in our energy field, causing blocks and stagnancy which then affects our lives, relationships and choices. When we step away from our inner dialogue and see our own hardships and trials as a mythic story, we can see that we played a part, but also no longer have to identify with that story. If we continue to identify with old, painful stories, we may be victimizing ourselves and impeding our growth. By first reclaiming them, empowering our story with the initiatory focus, then we are part of the bigger picture and give ourselves the room to grow beyond our smaller, limiting stories. We open ourselves up to a new way of living out our lives, using our power to shape our destiny, rather than our old stories.

Having support is crucial to the initiatory process. If we want to reframe a traumatic event in our lives, but had no community at the time, we can reclaim it, using the friendships and support we have now. If there is no support, then, as Chapter One suggests, form a women's circle or find a group of people with like minds who can help you reclaim your pain and turn it into power.

This is a much longer set of exercises than the other chapters simply because it is so important. I encourage you to spend time working with this process over the course of a few weeks or months so that you really do shift your awareness over past trauma into an empowered initiation. Even such dark issues as molestation, rape, and abuse can be viewed as initiations. In saying this, I in no way am rationalizing the actions of those who have caused such pain and suffering. But if we hold on to them as a way to continue to define us, then we are living as a victim and not an empowered woman. These deeper issues may require the guidance of a therapist or psychologist for further assistance in working through pain accumulated over many years. When working with the exercises below, I recommend beginning with an event that is simpler, one that you have somewhat healed from.

A Three-Part Process to Reclaim Initiation

Part One: Write It Down as a Fairy Tale

Fairy tales teach us of timelessness and transcend the normal boundaries of human experience. They are wonderful keys into our hidden subconscious world and can help to unlock our pain and turn it into power. By using symbols and writing the story as if we are watching from afar, we are also effectively healing the trauma and letting it go. It no longer becomes a drama to define ourselves with, but a mystical story that has given us gifts and insights to share with others.

To begin, read some myths and fairy tales for inspiration. Several myths are contained in this book. Also, think back over the fairy tales you grew up with, such as Cinderella and Little Red Riding Hood. I recommend Starhawk's presentation of "The Twelve Wild Swans" in her book *The Twelve Wild Swans* or some of the fairy tales told by Clarissa Pinkola Estés in *Women Who Run with the Wolves*. Once you have the idea, choose your initiatory experience, such as loss of a loved one, divorce, an illness, or an accident.

Writing a fairy tale will probably take some practice and this is as good a time to start as any. Start by making a clear outline of your story. It should have a beginning, a middle, and an end. When you write your outline, come up with symbols that represent the issue.

A dark, old woman who forces the fairy princess to suffer for days cleaning her home could symbolize an illness. A golden scroll with a message might be the finalized papers in a divorce. Some feathers from a magic goose could be the helping hand that appeared at the scene of an accident.

All fairy tales begin someplace. This is the initial setting, followed by the call to action, the hero's beginnings. Inanna begins her descent by putting on the necessary adornments. Cinderella's father is remarried and two new stepsisters move in with her. Describe the situation, but keep it simple and try to pick the images of the time that jump out at you. Was it autumn? What color did the fairy princess love to wear then? With whom did she live? Begin with the timeless phrase "Once upon a time…" and go from there, "…or not so long ago, there lived a beautiful young woman. She had hair the color of wood at sunset and eyes that glowed green."

The beginning is followed by a distinct change into the next phase of the tale, representing the initiation process itself. This should be the longest section of the story and may be a few pages. This is the diagnosis, the accident, or the breakup. The young woman gets married and leaves home; the appearance of a shadowy character comes into her life to teach her a lesson; the fairy princess is given a task to complete. This is the challenging part, the time in which the woman must overcome something. Again, try to think symbolically using actions. What did you go through to overcome this challenge? Write a task for the protagonist, such as sweeping out a house, turning stones into frogs, or cooking a stew for thousands. Make it difficult but not totally impossible.

Next, how did you face your fear? Choose some of the elements of the beginning to help the fairy princess face her task. For example, Cinderella's beauty becomes apparent only when she is dressed in dazzling clothes by her fairy godmother, yet she had this beauty all along! Did you have helpers along the way? Who helped you? Choose at least one person who helped you and symbolically place him or her in the story. Was she akin to a wolf, teaching you courage and stamina? Or was he more like a lizard whispering the power of dreams into your ear? For example, in my fairy tale, I used my husband, who is a warm, comforting bear, and nine sisters who give me necklaces to heal my broken heart. You may have had many helpers, but one or two will suffice. Finally, the task is complete, the fears have been faced.

The last section of the tale is the move into a completely new place. This is the start of something that is born of the task yet new and bright, healed and whole. The fairy princess and prince get married and move in together and she gives birth to a new daughter; the woman is healed; the house is closed up and sold for a new one. The ending must contain bits of the past, the event, the initiation in order to bear fruit. Hardships have been overcome and there is a clear reward, a benefit to the entire process. Treasures are found, and characters "live happily ever after."

After you have written your tale, you can revise it as necessary, add new sections, or illustrate it with images. The symbols you choose may very well begin to appear in your life in other ways, such as dreams or omens, and will become useful in helping you become the heroine in your own fairy tale life.

Part Two: Journey to the Underworld with Sound

The purpose of this exercise is to use the technique of journeying. For thousands of years, shamans, as the spiritual caretakers of the village, have used the journey process to aid in healing, divination, and counseling for the community. In its simplified form, the journey is a shift from the ordinary state of consciousness into the shamanic state of consciousness. This state of consciousness is akin to non-ordinary perception, which is a large spectrum of ways that we perceive the world, and can include (but is not limited to) intuition, messages from the other side such as ancestors or relatives, astral travel, communication with spirit guides or power animals, oracular dreams, visions during trance from repetitive sound or drumming, visions under the influence of psychotropic substances, and channeling. This is a varied list, yet we find that these altered conscious states are prevalent throughout the world, primarily in cultures where shamanic activity still takes place.

Journeying is an effective way to access our subconscious states, and I highly recommend it as a tool for healing and communication with spirits or other aspects of our selves. In my own experience, I have discovered connections between the subconscious or mystical realms and ordinary reality. For example, during a weekend workshop I saw a large "spirit" snake during one of the exercises. I danced as this snake, allowing it to move through me and feeling its wisdom. The next morning I walked to our meeting place in a roundabout way and, interestingly, found a snakeskin that had been shed during the night. This was just one small example of witnessing the external world reflecting back my own internal process, giving me a gift I could use to better understand the wisdom of the snake.

By using a drum or other repetitive sound, we can slip into this altered, non-ordinary perception more readily and receive the information needed. I have found, after leading journeys for others, that many people learn this method easily and can find out deeper information with just a little trust.

Setting an intention is a very important aspect of any kind of journey or healing work, perhaps the most important. By setting a clear intention, we are envisioning the path and intending that all the work we will be doing goes for the good of all, for the well-being of all involved. This helps to clear the way and allows guidance to come through and assist us using love. For the following journey, the intention is to ask for information regarding your initiation. Your intention is to revisit this experience as an observer, to gain information that may be useful to you now.

As with writing the fairy tale, first choose the initiatory event that you will be working with. Set up an altar and create a sacred circle, calling in the seven directions. Invite your guides, healing spirits, and ancestors to come into the circle to assist you in this process. For the sound element, either have someone do a steady drumbeat (a buffalo Native American frame drum is ideal) or use headphones and play a drumming CD. Use a recording that is created specifically for the journey process. Before you start, state in your mind your intention: "I intend to revisit my initiation and ask for any information that will help guide me now. I intend this in love and light."

Lie down and cover your eyes. Turn on the recording or have the drummer begin a steady drumbeat. Tell yourself that you are journeying to visit that point in your life, as an observer, as a second or third party. Watch as your memory goes back to that point. The drumbeat will allow you to revisit the time in an altered state. See if there is anything at that time that is important to you now. Ask your guides or higher self to show you anything that you need to know, receive, or communicate to others at that time. Trust the process as you move through this event. Send healing love and light to that moment in time, to the younger part of yourself that still remains unsettled by this event. Visualize golden light coming from present you (now), from your heart and hands, and pouring into younger or past you (then). Know that you are intimately connected, but that the pain no longer serves you now.

When you are finished, thank yourself and the others, the guides or other people who were part of this initiatory event in your life. Allow that to dissolve into a gift that you receive and put in your pocket. This may come in the form of an animal, crystal, scroll, or beam of light. As the drumming begins to slow down, intend that you return to yourself now, in your body, whole and healed. Feel the gratitude in your heart for your experience and take time to come back.

When you are ready, sit up and write down your experience. Writing it immediately, at its freshest, keeps the message of the journey stronger within you. If you want to, share the journey with the other people in your group or with the drummer. Remember, though, that the information is sacred and the gift may be a medicine that is not to be told to everyone. Receiving spirit medicine is an honor, and by keeping that quiet, we allow the power to grow stronger within. When you feel ready, thank the directions and close the circle.

Part Three: Revisit through Healing Work with a Witness

This is the final step in reclaiming your initiatory experience. This must be done with at least one other person as the witness to the event. Similar to the journey, it revisits the initiatory experience and aims to heal it and bring back any gifts. It can also be combined with the journey using drums.

Prepare for this journey by choosing which experience you will revisit and call to mind details from that time. You must feel comfortable enough to say this aloud, so the witness (and any others you wish to be present) must be someone you feel completely open with. You must also feel safe, and healing work can be done (such as Reiki, massage, journal work) to prepare you for the experience.

Prepare the room by setting up a mat on the floor or a massage table, creating an altar of healing images, lighting a candle, and calling in sacred space. When you are ready, lie down. The witness should then take some time to have everyone present (including you) call in their guides, ancestors, or higher spirit and set the intention that this practice be done in love and light. The witness then covers your eyes and reminds you that *you* are the one who is reclaiming your initiation, that you are empowering yourself. The witness, like the genderless spirits from Inanna's descent, is simply witnessing the pain of the initiate, allowing you to heal.

The witness then gently tells you to deeply relax. Relax your entire body, part by part. This is to facilitate an altered state that will allow you to revisit the experience without so much emotion to overwhelm you. This should take at least ten minutes. No need to rush. Then the witness tells you to go back to the time just before the event (the accident, divorce, illness, trauma). The witness reminds you that you are being held with love and guidance and asks you to see if anyone or any being is there who is assisting you through the process. Begin speaking when you are ready and narrate the story with a beginning, middle, and end. You should speak in the present tense, as if indeed you are walking yourself through the experience. As an initiate, be open to anything revelatory that may arise during this process.

The witness remains quiet and takes notes as you tell your story. For example, you might say, "I am in my house and I receive the call from the doctor. He tells me I have cancer. I am very sad and overwhelmed, but my friends are coming now, to hold me and support me. I am not alone." When you speak of your pain, the witness should mirror that pain back to you, saying "I understand. I am holding you. I am here." This is the most delicate aspect of the process and may take some practice on the part of the witness to perfect. If you have no training in the healing arts, counseling, etc., I recommend that you practice this role with someone first using a positive or mundane experience before moving into the place of initiatory work. This being said, if you are working with the same group of women over time, the comfort level is strong and the initiate will feel supported.

The witness follows you through your story, noting down important things and reflecting your pain, thus taking some of it and helping to dissolve it. Other aspects of this process may come up. For example, when I was doing this with a friend who was adopted, she felt moved to dialogue with her mother who had given her up for adoption so many years ago. I held the space and asked her questions like, "What does your mother say to you, as an infant?" and "What do you want to tell your mother?" This was a very powerful healing as she saw how her mother had no other choice, but loved her immensely. This allowed my friend to move through the feelings of abandonment and resolve some of that pain.

When you have finished the narration, the witness helps you send healing back to that time. Visualize a golden light emanating from you now and shining back to the time of that event. Do this for several minutes. Finally, if there were any noticeable guides during the process, or if any other people were important, thank them and also send them love and light. This is also the moment to ask if there are any gifts, as sometimes a symbolic image is given which you can take to use in your own path of power.

When this is finished, slowly come back to consciousness by breathing deeply into your belly and becoming aware of your surroundings. Rest for a while, then slowly sit up and drink some clear, fresh water. When you are ready, you may talk about your experience some and relive a few of the moments. The witness can also offer her feedback, but only in relation to the initiate's experience, using the notes she took or repeating what was said. There is no need for advice or counsel here, just support and reflection. The witness should now ask you to come up with an affirmation that helps you to ground the shift and love you have felt into words. This may be something like "I share my power with love," or "I am clear and whole." The witness should also ask if there is something you feel you need to do in the coming weeks, perhaps a ritual or ceremony to honor this transition. This can be as simple as sitting with a candle in gratitude or visiting a body of water to reflect on your process. It is important that you come up with the ritual and affirmation on your own, with the help of the witness, so that you are truly reclaiming the initiation yourself.

Finally, when all feel the process is complete, thank the guides and ancestors for their blessing. Close the circle and release the directions. Perhaps eat some nourishing food to ground after the ceremony and connect with each other. You may feel you'd like to do the follow-up ritual or ceremony by yourself or with others and those plans can be set at the closing of the circle.

Reclaiming Menarche Ceremony

By re-membering our menses as a sacred function in our body, we are not only getting in touch with our own inner female wisdom, we are transmuting something thought of as impure into power. Revisiting your first menses, or menarche, is a good step to reclaim the power in your own body.

First, make an altar to honor the first blood time in your life, when wisdom began to flow through you, through your womb. Perhaps put a photo of yourself at that age, things you loved then, animals you felt drawn to, and women you looked up to at that time in your life. Other items to honor that time might include red candles, incense, and images of a feminine quality that speaks to you of coming power and womanhood. Spend a few days preparing the altar, as you are honoring a huge transition in your life, one that may have been hardly celebrated, dismissed, or even thought of as negative. Nourish the young girl who was looking to others for help; imagine you are reaching back to her and creating a space for her that is sacred.

Find some time when you can be alone (or with a group of trusted women) and create sacred space around your altar. Call in your guides and any women who nurtured you in the past or are nurturing you now. Then write about the experience and everything you felt at the time. If you are like many women in Western culture, probably not much happened in an honoring way, and, even worse, you may have been told things that made you feel ashamed for starting to bleed. Use the journal time to release those memories, to let them air onto paper. Put the story on the altar and tell it aloud if you wish, to the women in the circle or simply to yourself.

Next, take some time to send healing and love back to yourself as a girl, preteen, or teenager, whenever you first bled. Lie down and have someone drum for you if you wish, or give you some laying on of hands healing so that you are in a relaxed state. Imagine you are slowly descending down ten steps into a garden, relaxing deeply on each step. Once you have reached the bottom of the steps, go through a door and into the garden. Spend some time relaxing and healing here. Then visualize that time in your life when you first discovered your period, seeing the blood in your underwear. What were the first feelings that you had? Were you excited, ashamed, afraid? Imagine you are assisting that young girl through that time, sending your healing light back to her and her discovery.

Then visualize sitting with your younger self before a campfire. Imagine your mother and your grandmother also with you at the fire. Tell the women of your lineage how you feel about becoming a woman. Allow each of them to speak to you as well, feeling them from their true selves, giving you love and encouragement. Speak any unvoiced issues that are surrounding this time in your life. Ask for healing and reclaiming from your guides and let the love flow into your womb and heart.

When you feel finished, thank your mother and grandmother. Rest for a while in your garden, perhaps in water to cleanse and purify yourself. Then slowly come back into normal consciousness by the drum slowing down and by visualizing climbing up the stairs, counting back up to ten. Take some time to sit up slowly, drink some water, and then write down what you have experienced. Share with the other women in the circle.

If you have a daughter, I highly recommend that you help her design a ceremony for her own first menses at that time. We all have the inherent capability to create ritual and it can be as simple as sitting with your daughter, lighting a candle, and welcoming her to womanhood or as elaborate as having her dress in white, singing songs with the community and dancing her way through a decorated gateway symbolizing becoming a woman. This will provide acknowledgement for your daughter as she transitions from girl to adolescent and will support her process. Even something very simple will give your daughter something to remember in the years to come, a seed of light that honors her power as she grows into womanhood.

THREE

THE WARRIORESS
Cultivating the Tools of Empowerment

The warrior is a person who walks the path impeccably,
one who knows with clarity the proper use of energy.
A warrior chooses a path with heart,
any path with heart, and follows it;
and then he rejoices and laughs.
He knows because he sees that his life will be
over altogether too soon. He sees that nothing is more
important than anything else.

—CARLOS CASTANEDA

Imagine yourself emerging, like Inanna, from the depths of
the darkness below. An overwhelming sense of confidence
moves through you, electrifying your body, heart, and mind.
You are born again, renewed and whole; cleansed and revi-
talized by the process of reclaiming your inner power. As you
climb up and out of the depths of the cavern, onto the bottom
of the canyon, you realize that even more gifts await you. As
you reach the canyon floor, you see your inner Warrioress as

*a goddess or strong woman waiting for you, standing proud
under a tree that glows. She leads you to the tree and performs a sacred dance around you, imbuing you with power
as energy streams through your body. She hands you tools
that represent your power. One of the sacred tools is a mask
of an animal; this is your personal guardian and power
animal that will assist you on the climb, flight, or dance up
the canyon to reach your inner garden that awaits. As you
begin your climb, you smile. The sun is brilliant, the sky
endless blue, and your heart sings as you know that you are
not alone, that you are power-full.*

Once we have reclaimed our power through initiation, we are ready
to embrace our inner Warrioress, the one who helps us by firmly
holding our power in place. The Warrioress does not back down
from those people or past events that seek to suppress or oppress
her. She is comfortable with the dark mother and her shadow;
she can effectively turn pain into power and is gleeful to do so. An
empowered Warrioress has overcome her abuse, her violations of
the past, her trauma, her illness, and been restored victorious. The
Warrioress here comes in the form of Artemis, the moon goddess of
the hunt who runs with wild abandon in virgin forests. She teaches
us the power to say no and set clear boundaries and guides us to call
even more power into our lives.

The Warrioress honors her intuitive voice and does not bow
down to the "nice girl" projections that are pervasive in our culture.
In other words, if a young woman who is expected to follow certain
social rules, being a good, productive daughter, instead leaves home,
rides a train across America with only a hundred dollars in her
pocket, and risks everything to start a new life, you can imagine the
Warrioress had something to do with that. The Warrioress mani-
fested in my great-grandmother who, according to family legend,

left Hungary because she wasn't allowed to dance. She made her way to Italy and met up with a family who brought her to America! In America she danced, had children, and created a completely new life for herself, remaining quite feisty throughout her life and passing on at the ripe old age of 104. Her long white hair, sharp eyes, and peculiar manner of speaking left an indelible imprint on my young self. Every family certainly has its rebel black sheep and women who have boldly tried something new.

Even amidst the most repressed of social mores, we find the Warrioress. I was pleased to learn that the first Western people to turn the addictive and stimulating cocoa drink of the Mayans into a sweet and milky delight was a group of French Catholic nuns! They became so enamored of it that even the ban that was put into place by the Vatican was completely ignored by those chocolate-loving nuns. The Warrioress has a wondrous sense of humor as well.

Sometimes, Warrioress power is mistaken for the negative feminine such as the wily bitch or the voracious whore. These roles are played out time and time again in contemporary stories but have roots in a distant past. There is a strange image from history that illuminates the fear of woman power, the *vagina dentate*. This peculiar icon of a toothed vagina that lurks in corners, waiting to seduce men, and then bite down unexpectedly was used by medieval Christianity to symbolize the gates of hell. This is an especially disturbing aspect of the shadow time when women were seen as being in consort with the devil. I think a reclaiming of such an image might just boost our inner Warrioress; I am envisioning a t-shirt with a toothed vagina and the saying, "No more nice girl." Imagine for a moment if our vaginas *did* have teeth, such as retractable teeth that could be extended at will. Rape would certainly disappear![8] This feisty quality in women is often still demonized today. We all know the local woman who drinks too much, engages in "inappropriate" sex, comes up with wild and glamorous schemes—in essence embodies the potentiated creative force. This kind of woman is often made a scapegoat. I have seen a modern-day form of witch burning happen several times in places I have lived, where the wild actions of these women were both intensely attractive and repulsive to the people around her. If something goes awry in the community, you can bet she is there, the Warrioress, the slicer of illusions, wreaking havoc and reminding us of those very un–good girl qualities that reside in each of us.

Saying No

Sometimes, to remain true to the power of the Warrioress, we have to say no. As women, many of us fall into the pattern of fearing the outcome if we say no. We may be worried or anxious about how others will react if we say no to the various demands that our family, friends, and community ask of us. Yet, we cannot truly own and work from a place of power until we learn how to say no. We are blessed to live in a country where we are mostly free to choose what we want to do with our lives, careers, relationships, and spiritual development; many women around the world do not have these opportunities. Thus, we have an even greater responsibility to choose things that empower and nourish us.

---

8. Since writing this, I have discovered that a woman has actually developed a toothed condom to put inside a woman's vagina as protection against the high rates of rape in South Africa. When I wrote this, it was months before this story surfaced, but it is interesting to note that perhaps there is more to this image after all. See http://articles.cnn.com/2010-06-20/world/south.africa .female.condom for more.

Often we become attached to our way of doing a myriad of activities and then identify ourselves as the one who provides things for everyone else. For example, I often prepare and host ceremonies and circles for the moons, seasons, and celebratory events. Sometimes I am overwhelmed by this work, although it is very natural for me to do it; sometimes I have to simply *not act* on my impulse to always create ceremony for others so that I have energy for my own internal work and my writing. Loosening our attachments or compulsions and feeling we must act is necessary to grow the power of the Warrioress within. Part of this is recognizing that life carries on just fine without our input. If we can step back from that impulse to act, we can allow ourselves to rest for a moment. Bringing this spaciousness into our days inevitably empowers us to then act with clarity and strength rather than from a place of neediness, compulsion, or fear of hurting others' feelings.

The Warrioress is brilliant in her power and does not care what others think. This may sound harsh, yet we actually benefit more people by coming from an empowered space which illuminates our relationships rather than draining them. Part of this process of becoming powerful is recognizing the people who assist in our development and those who may not benefit us. Just as we might stop eating certain foods that do not feel good in our body, we may want to set intentions to peacefully dissolve relations that do not nourish us. Yet, we must realize that this dissolution is temporary; we cannot simply cancel out all things that we perceive as harmful. But once we regain our strength and our inner Warrioress, we can work from a place that comes from pure, clear awareness and can then meet all kinds of obstacles

EXERCISE 3.1

Boundary Circle

This is a simple exercise that visually helps you see who and what is really crucial to your life. Draw a circle on a piece of blank paper.

Inside the circle, write down the people and activities you feel currently committed to. Outside the circle, write down the people and things you feel are draining and not nourishing you. This also enables you to see who and what you are giving your energy to. The purpose of this exercise is to help you see and clarify what is in your life and better choose things that are empowering. Often we spend time with people or doing things that are not totally fulfilling. It is important to remember this is a temporary circle, not something that defines you for the rest of your life. Some of the people and things outside of the circle will inevitably be part of your circle once again; perhaps you simply need a breather. After a few weeks, you can burn the circle and create a new one as you see fit. Use the circles to refine what it is in your life that you really want to focus on. The more energy you put toward the people and activities within your circle, the more empowered you will feel.

Artemis

The worship of Artemis dates from deep in our ancient history, as long ago as the Paleolithic (circa 10,000 BCE). She was originally worshipped as the goddess of the wild animals and is the deity with the oldest roots among the Greek gods and goddesses. Her name is not Greek but comes from the Mycenaean language and Minoan goddesses of Crete. Original statues of Artemis depict massive wings, linking her to the bird goddesses. Artemis was often carved out of black stone and displayed many breasts, a dark mother portraying her multitude of qualities including power and nourishment. She was associated with the hunt and was often portrayed with hunting dogs. She was also connected to the Great She-Bear, which is found in the night sky as Ursa Major. Her devotion to wilderness and her vow to never marry are inspiring to our own inner Warrioress.

Artemis of the Wild

Artemis was born to her powerful father Zeus and beautiful mother Leto, a mistress of Zeus. She was the first-born of twins. After her birth, Artemis aided her mother in her nine-day struggle to give birth to her twin brother, Apollo. Artemis experienced the fear and power associated with birth and knew she did not want to have children of her own.

Artemis grew into a beautiful and strong girl. Her face shone with power and grace, just like the moon she ruled over. When Artemis was three, Zeus asked her what she wanted most, and she replied, "I want the wilderness as my special place, a bow and arrow to hunt with, a short tunic to run in, a band of nymphs to accompany me, a pack of hounds, and to never, ever get married." Zeus, impressed with her zeal and directness, granted her the gifts of a huntress and promised that she would remain unmarried for all of her life.

When Artemis was full grown, she loved to run wild in the forests. She was often seen with a deer or stag and knew intimately the power of the hunter as well as the fear of being hunted. Sometimes Artemis took the role of the great bear protector or the wild boar destroyer. She loved the wilderness so dearly and took great care that no one harmed or tainted its natural beauty.

One day Artemis was bathing nude in one of her favorite streams. The hunter Actaeon crept up through the foliage and spotted the beautiful naked goddess, water streaming over her body. Artemis enjoyed her bath for a few more minutes but knew instantly she was being watched. Suddenly she turned around and with a fierce and wild look in her eye she transformed Actaeon into a stag. Frightened, the stag Actaeon fled. Artemis commanded his own hounds to chase him, and they pursued him over hills and valleys until they caught him and viciously tore him to pieces. Artemis smiled at her own unmaking of the insensitive hunter and finished her bath.

Keys to the Tale

Artemis was known as the "lady of the wild mountains," the goddess of the wildest places both in nature and in our hearts. She is the goddess of the moon and the night, shining down onto the dense forests that once covered the earth, illuminating the forest floor and its creatures that lived there. She is distinctly connected with the wild animals and beasts and often portrayed walking with a stag or a doe or even appearing herself as a great mother bear with her baby. She is the guardian of the most remote places, the lonely mountain tops, the meadows filled with wildflowers, the roaring streams in uninhabited forests, and the darkness of night and clarity of a star-filled sky. Artemis is a pure Warrioress, clear in her intent and wild in her ambitions.

Paradoxically, Artemis, who never gave birth to her own children, was also the goddess of childbirth. This was because she helped her mother for nine days to birth her twin brother. She gained intimate experience with the process of childbirth and was called upon by women in ancient Greece to assist them in their own labors. Artemis was extremely young when she helped her mother (just after her own birth) and was given the immense responsibility of assisting birth. Many of us, as young girls, have also been given responsibility that seemed overwhelming, such as caring for younger children, protecting ourselves or others from negative or traumatic family situations, or perhaps an understanding of the world that may have seemed frightening for our young years. This is not uncommon for girl children, who are often exposed to grown-up issues earlier than boys. Reaching back and reclaiming our own traumas and reframing them as gifts or powers imbued upon us is an important way to empower our inner selves. Just as we explored reclaiming an initiation, I encourage you to also work on the reclaiming of hard lessons learned as a young child.

You can use the same methods in Chapter Two to transform what you may perceive as a negative childhood experience into a powerful gift that, like Artemis, can be used to help yourself as well as other women.

Artemis, at the tender age of three, makes very specific requests from her father. She asks for the wilderness, a bow and arrow, a short tunic, a band of nymphs, a pack of hounds, and, most importantly, to remain unmarried. Artemis is the sacred maiden or virgin goddess, a powerful aspect of our inner Warrioress. The true meaning of the word *virgin*, according to the research of Sjöö and Mor, is that "ancient moon priestesses were called virgins. 'Virgin' meant not married, not belonging to a man—a woman who was 'one-in-herself.' The very word derives from a Latin root meaning strength, force, skill…Ishtar, Diana, Astarte, Isis were all called virgins, which did not refer to sexual chastity, but sexual independence."[9] Artemis represents that clear, untouched part, the virgin territory, the unclaimed spirit that resides within each of us regardless of what has happened in our lives. This is crucial in our reclaiming process, to revisit this powerful part that yearns to be in connection with our wildness, our instinctive self. This is also a reminder that, like Artemis, we don't really need a partner. That does not mean a partner doesn't enhance our life in beautiful and strengthening ways, as my own husband does for me, but we are powerful on our own terms. Looking inward for resources, rather than outward for validation, empowers us.

Artemis explores her wilderness sometimes with her pack of hounds and other times with a deer or stag. This symbolizes both the hunted and the hunter; thus she is paradoxical in nature. Artemis reflects the double-edged sword of sacrifice and pursuit. Knowing the balance of these two qualities is part of the power of the Warrioress. Sometimes we must sacrifice aspects of our inner

---

9.   Sjöö and Mor, p. 158.

desires for the well-being of our family, children, and community. But at other times, we need to maintain what is right for us and nourishes our own power and stay true to that, regardless of others' views. Cultivating the quality of discernment enables us to know when to act and when to sacrifice aspects of our selves for the whole.

In one of Artemis's most famous stories, she turns the hunter Actaeon into a stag to be hunted by his own hounds. Although it might seem outrageous, a violent goddess tearing a man to pieces to protect her own chastity, we can find a well of inspiration from this small but potent story. The Warrioress is evident here, in that she is not only defending herself from prying eyes, she is giving the peeper a taste of his own medicine. Sometimes this kind of ferocity is of utmost importance in a world that continues to oppress the feminine, women, and children. Although we are making progress in undoing the damage of the last several millennia, on a global scale women are still targets for hideous crimes such as rape camps, sex trafficking, bride burning, obscene pornography such as snuff films, and so on. In fact, it is important to fire up the inner Warrioress at times and take action against these crimes. Each year more women and children are sold into sexual slavery than the entire number of people sold during the trans-Atlantic slave trade of a hundred years! Some ways we can make change are to donate to organizations working on women's issues; incorporate healing of these situations into our ceremonies; stand up and defend ourselves when we are harassed verbally or physically; teach our daughters how to be fearless and teach our sons how to honor women. We can make magic with our sacred feminine power and become the change we wish to see.

In her book *Awakening the Warrior Within*, Dawn Callan discusses the reality that when a woman is victimized or raped, there is an energy at work from both sides. I am in no way suggesting that a woman is responsible for an attack or rape, but I am saying that after thousands of years of abuse and oppression the mentality of victimhood may be hardwired into our minds and bodies. Callan comments on the fact that many women in her workshops heard a voice coming into their head saying something like, "Just let it happen, it'll be over soon" when they were attacked. This may seem shocking, yet this has happened to countless women as well as men. Just as we must work to reframe trauma into power, we must also retrain our minds so that in serious incidents, our reaction is not one of quiet submission, but rather fierce reaction. Just as Artemis uses her infinite power to destroy Actaeon, we too can stand up for what is right. Using our inner Warrioress provides the opportunity to act power-filled, even if it means standing fierce and wild, not necessarily pleasing others, or always being so kind.

Artemis was often depicted in the form of the Great Bear, a fierce animal who also lovingly suckles its infants. In ancient Greece, young women performed dances for Artemis wearing bear masks to honor her fierce power. In shamanic cultures it is believed that we are all empowered by one or more animal guides that work as personal totems or guardians. Traditional cultures use the guardian spirit for strength to carry us through the pain of life. Additional guardian spirits are discovered during the time of initiation such as a vision quest or a menses ceremony. In today's fast-paced, mechanistic world, we may be disconnected from our nature and our power source. From the shamanic perspective, depression, fear, alienation, and illness, all common symptoms of modern society, result from a loss of power and even soul loss. By reconnecting with our guardian spirit animal, we call in power that serves as protection and kindles the fire of our inner Warrioress. Connecting our subconscious with a guardian spirit or power animal sends a clear message to our conscious mind that we are fearless and know the right action as Warrioress in different stages of our life.

Finding a Guardian Spirit

This exercise enables you to reclaim a guide or power animal and helps you get in touch with your animal-like nature. If we look around us, we see that animals are in harmony with their world. They do not over-consume or make vast amounts of useless products to "ease" their lifestyle. They simply breathe, eat, live, and if nature forces them to change, they evolve. We, especially in Western culture, still have a lot to relearn about deeply connecting with animals. When we look at ancient history, we find not only Artemis but many gods and goddesses who are associated with animals and their aspects. These animals are not just symbolic; they are used as omens, guides, and messengers between the realms. For example, the eagle may symbolize the east or new ideas and the ability to see the big picture, as well as offering guidance on how to begin something new or which direction to follow in life.

You may have different kinds of guardians, spirit guides, as well as your ancestors, such as the ones you connected with in Exercise 2.1. However, connecting with an animal guide can really help you tap your power as well as helping to protect you. Although it may seem that the animal is an aspect of you—and certainly it is on some level—still these guardians have a very real presence in your life once you connect with them and should be treated with respect. You may have significant dreams about them, see or find parts of them in nature, or simply have the sense that they are with you. You can honor their presence by building an altar to them, painting a picture, or dancing to celebrate their power.

Guardian spirits enter our lives and work with us in specific ways: as a totem that is with us throughout life, as a medicine animal that comes for a shorter time for a specific reason, and as a direct connection to our natural environment. A totem or lifelong guardian spirit is often an animal that we have felt a kinship for a long time with, perhaps since our childhood. When I was little, I was obsessed with collecting owl figurines and grew up surrounded by this image—a fitting goddess image, I was to discover much later. A guardian spirit that comes into our life for a shorter period of time helps us during transitions and gives us specific medicine or power for that time. For example, we may be grieving the loss of a loved one and find that the warmth of mother bear and her instinct to hibernate comforts our inner psyche. Another way a power animal might appear in our lives is one that is associated with visionary power, and directly connected with the natural world we live in. In the weeks just before I moved to Hawai'i, I had two dreams of a white hawk that came to bless me and give me specific information. Upon arriving in the islands, I noticed a hawk, called 'io in native Hawai'ian, that is white when it is young. We named our house 'Io Estate, and two days after this naming, three hawks turned up and perched in the yard for a few hours.

To connect with your guardian spirit, first set up your altar and create sacred space. Perhaps include an image of Artemis, the Lady of the Beasts, or other images that represent a connection to the animal and creature realms. Light candles and burn some incense if you like. You may wish to do this exercise alone or with a group. Lie down and slowly relax your body, one body part at a time, by saying either out loud softly or in your mind, "I relax my feet...my feet are completely relaxed," and so on with each part of the body, including your organs, all the way up to the top of your head. In doing this, you are able to sink into an altered state of consciousness. This can also be achieved through drumming or repetitive sound. You can have someone in a group situation lead the visualization, tape this section and play it back, or simply remember it and follow it in your mind.

Your body is deeply relaxed. Now visualize that you are at the top of a flight of stairs going down. State in your mind your intention to go down into the lower realm to find a guardian spirit.

Descend down the stairs slowly, counting backwards from ten to one. As you reach one, there will be a door. Go through the door and into a garden. Spend some time in this garden; notice the flowers, the trees, the light, and the smells. Wander around the garden, feeling the soft breeze on your skin and the warmth of the sun or coolness of the night. Notice a body of water in the garden, a stream or pond or fountain. Refresh yourself for a while there, letting all your cares wash away in the cool water, then lie in the sun, completely relaxed and rejuvenated. After some time, get up and walk toward a field.

As you approach the center of the field, you will be met by a guardian spirit or power animal. Feel the presence of this spirit and be open to any messages from your guardian. A message may come audibly, visually, or through knowing. Be open to receiving a gift from your guardian spirit such as an object, a dance,, or song. You may feel the need to play or explore this realm with your animal. You nan do so, or you can return to find out more information as needed. When you are finished, make sure to thank your guardian and send back love in gratitude.

Then return to your garden and revisit the water for a moment, then the flowers, trees, and everything else there. When you are ready, start to come back to the door and go through. Count back up to ten, climbing the stairs one at a time. When you reach the top, slowly come back into normal consciousness, stretching your body and slowly sitting up. Write down what you have experienced and remember the guardian spirit has now made contact with you.

This is only one way to visit a guardian spirit in the lower realms. I was trained in my shamanic studies to retrieve a power animal using the steady beat of a drum to alter my consciousness. Experiment until you find what works for you. It is also important to keep in mind that some people do not "see" anything on the journey, but have more of a knowing, a feeling or sensation. Others may hear something, such as voices or songs or instruments that give information. This is all part of the process of learning to trust and use your intuitive voice. Once you have established contact with your guardian, signs may appear to connect you to your spirit. You might encounter the animal or bird you met, or you may dream of this spirit guide. Remember to honor and nourish the connection by dancing the spirit, building an altar, and continuing to journey to the guardian for further information.

Masked Dance Ceremony

This ceremony is an act of power and a way to honor your guardian spirit and draw in further protection. Traditionally, cultures have performed masked dances to gather power, consult oracles or cast divinations, and celebrate the major turning points of life in a village. The mask is a way to dissolve your smaller self and grow powerfully into spirit. When you put on your mask, the person or identities that you habitually create dissolve, and a powerful, archetypal self emerges, infused by the energy of the guardian spirit.

Before beginning the ceremony, set aside time to create your mask. This project is even more fun with your women's group and can be incorporated into one of your gatherings. You can make a mask in several ways. One way is to use simple paper materials with string to attach it. Another way is to use embedded plaster strips. You can buy the strips at any local art store. You must make this kind of mask with at least one other person who can form the mask on your face. This mask feels even more powerful because it will fit your face perfectly. Simply follow the directions on the package for first cutting the strips, then wetting them and laying them across the person's face. After the mask dries, decorate it with paint, glitter, feathers, jewelry, clay, or any material you see fit to express your guardian spirit.

The ceremony can be done any time of the year and is nice to do under a waxing or full moon so the power of the moon enhances the dance. Gather together the following items: your mask(s); four candles for the four cardinal directions or wood for an outdoor fire if that is possible; offerings for the four directions as well as offerings for mother earth, father sky, and center; drums and rhythm makers.

The ceremony is very simple after you have prepared your mask. If you are doing this ceremony outside, first prepare the fire. Have one person (or more) be the drummer or sound maker for the ceremony. You can also provide rattles and drums for each person in the group or have them bring their own. If it is only you, then use a drumming CD or your own sound maker for this ceremony.

Next, call in the directions and create sacred space. If you are having a fire, stand around the fire in a circle and call in the seven directions of east, south, west, north, mother earth, father sky, and center and give offerings. If there is no fire, then use the four candles and give offerings to all seven directions. If it is a larger group, you may have one person for each direction, or perhaps two or three different people assigned to two or more directions. Once the directions have been called, then create sacred space, visualizing an area large enough for the dance surrounded by brilliant blue circle.

The drummers then start to beat a slow drumbeat. Everyone puts on their mask and begins to move to the drumbeat. At the moment that you put on the mask, simply send out the intention to call in your guardian spirit to your body. Open your body to receiving your guardian spirit and dancing this source of power. Slowly the drumbeat speeds up. People can pick up their own rattles, drums, or sound makers and make sound as they begin to move around the fire. The dance continues for a half hour or more, depending on the music makers. Feel the energy of your guardian flowing through you as you dance and move and bring the power of this animal through you. Notice the other dancers with their masks and how they transform in the firelight.

After a long session of dancing, the drummers slow the beat as you integrate yourself back into the present moment. Thank the guardian spirit and then lie down to receive any further messages from the spirit. The drummer can continue drumming as you open to feeling the power move through you, connecting you to both earth and spirit.

The drummer finally stops and there are several moments of silence. Each of the direction callers thanks the directions, releases them, and dissolves the sacred space. Finally, remove your mask and hold it against your heart. Feel the power move through you over the next day and pay attention to your dreams, where you are often visited by your guardian spirits.

FOUR

THE HEALER
Birthing and Growing

I, the fiery life of divine wisdom,
I ignite the beauty of the plains,
I sparkle the waters,
I burn in the sun, and the moon, and the stars,
With wisdom I order all rightly...
I adorn all the Earth,
I am the breeze that nurtures all things green...
I am the rain coming from the dew
That causes the grasses to laugh with the joy of life.
I call forth the tears, the aroma of holy work.
I am the yearning for good.
—HILDEGARD OF BINGEN

Imagine that you have made your way up the canyon and
arrived at the top. You are holding the immense inner power
of the sacred feminine and ready to open to the soft, gentle
caress of love. As you crest the final steps of the canyon, you
come upon a large meadow filled with flowers and trees.

*There awaits your beautiful, shimmering sacred garden.
This is your own creative garden, which you can arrange
as it suits you. This is a place of healing, a place to return
to when you need nourishment. As you walk through the
meadow and garden, observing the stones and flowers, you
come to a beautiful stream lined with colored pebbles. You
wade up the stream until it becomes a deep, emerald green
pool. The water is cool and refreshing. A small waterfall
runs into the pond and the sound of rushing water soothes
you and begins to heal you from your journey to the depths
and your return. A beautiful woman sits on a rock next
to the stream. She is the mirror of your inner healer, the
watery spirit that breathes love into your being.*

The Healer is the cleansing that occurs after the intense shifts of
calling in the power of the sacred feminine. We have climbed up
from the abyss, made our way out of the underworld fueled by our
inner power and into the nourishing and expansive realms of love.
After descending down, meeting with our inner spirit and the fire
of transformation, we are ready for the flow of the Healer's water
to wash over us, to let our tears become a voice and heal us with
watery wisdom. The Healer visits us in the form of the mother
earth and her waters. Mami Wata, the wild and powerful African
mermaid of oceans and rivers, is the Healer who blesses us with her
ancient knowledge of the vital life forces on earth.

The Healer is deeply connected to the mother, the quality in
us that receives the creative seeds, grows life, and births forms of
beauty. She may be the literal mother of children, or the mother of
ideas, an emotion, an artwork, a company. The Healer is found in
the healing of mother earth and gives us the gifts of potent medicine in the form of plants, animals, waters, soils, and minerals of her
body.

The Healer is the nurturing part of us that knows when to hold our children close, listen to a friend over tea, weed the garden and plant new herbs for our cooking, lay hands on those who are emotionally troubled or wounded. She is the part of us that effortlessly renews our body and regenerates our cells. She is the midwife who births new projects, healing, babies, ideas, and healed bodies. She is the wonderful balm to all of our sores and afflictions, who can remind us that peace and love are inherent in all things. When we open ourselves to our inner Healer, we become like pure, clear water, capable of moving effortlessly through the world.

Our Body as a Planet

Our home is the earth. The earth provides us with everything we need: all our food, clothing, resources. Everything we use comes from the earth; in this way she is truly like a mother. Many indigenous creation stories speak of the great mother who gave birth to all things or split herself into pieces to form the earth. From the earth grow all the living things, including sacred plants that abound for our delight to use for food, healing, and medicine. Many of those uses are now being reclaimed as we reconnect to the lost arts of working with herbs, fruits, barks, and plants in healing.

Traditional cultures recognize that spiritual sustenance, as well as physical, comes from the earth herself. In various parts of South America, people are intimately connected to the spiritual qualities of plants. Several of these plants are considered to be healing aspects of the sacred feminine, including ayahuasca, a psychotropic plant that provides healing visions through shamanic ceremony. The cultures who use ayahuasca believe it is imbued with a feminine spirit that enables the healing. In certain cultures, at birth the umbilical cord is packed with small amounts of ayahuasca, so the newborn can begin his or her direct connection to mother earth, known as Pachamama. This connection to the earth promotes a deep sense of belonging and connectedness to the natural world.

We can feel our own connection to the earth when we are in nature. For example, when we visit an incredible natural place such as the Grand Canyon, we admire its magnificence and grandeur. We are compelled by the rawness of age and its effect on the rock and earth that have, over the course of millions of years, been worn away by a single river! When we visit places where glaciers have cut away mountains, leaving behind formations, we admire them, take photographs, and tell stories. Our bodies are a reflection of these planetary processes: they grow, they shift, they change, they decay, they die, then are born again, as soil, sunflowers, or oak trees. Our inner Healer enables us to view our own bodies as a planet of change, power, and natural beauty.

Viewing our bodies as a planet is a positive first step in cultivating inner nourishment and self-love. This will help us to dissolve some of our cultural attachments to beauty and physical appearances. We are surrounded by media and culture that values permanent youth, physical perfection, ultra-white teeth, and flawless skin. These images are the antithesis of death, blackness, decay, and even birth, qualities long associated with the goddess and her power. When it comes to the decay of our bodies, to our own canyons that form on our faces, to the formations that seem to pop up all over our skin as we age, many of us worry over it, hate the aging and work to hide it, or use chemicals or surgery to defy it.

I have a fantastic photo of an old woman in Ladakh, who has lived in some of the highest mountains on earth her entire life. She has probably only looked in a mirror a few times, on her wedding day perhaps, many decades ago. Her face is as brown and wrinkled as a walnut and she has only a few teeth. She is smiling a smile that moves throughout her entire body; she is caught in mid-laugh, her dark brown eyes sparkling like a million suns. Every woman who sees that picture sighs and says, "Wow. She is amazing." Why do we say this? Because we still remember that even though image after image in the media continues to propagate a particular brand of beauty, the dark mother, the woman of the earth, the voice of the goddess is a source of beauty that nourishes our souls.

I am calling out for a revision to the notion that we must look smooth, white (or perfectly tanned), flawless, arched in heels, and made up to be considered beautiful, professional, powerful. Take time to sit and ask yourself about some of these practices. We have the freedom in this country to question our physical identities. For example, you may want to ask yourself, "Why, really, do I wear high heels? They make my legs and butt 'look better' but to whom?" Why do we continue to perpetuate a custom that contorts our spines, hurts our feet, and pinches our toes? How is this custom really that different from customs we now perceive as horrible, such as foot binding, corsets, or metal girdles? We can ask this about many things, such as shaving, bras, makeup, and fingernail polish. I am not saying we should abandon self-adornment, but I do think we need to ask ourselves a little more deeply, *why* do I do this? If we have been told to do it by the culture, how then does that empower us? We may find pleasure in these things—many women do, and I understand that. I too like getting waxed and putting color on my eyes. Yet, I do feel it is important to reflect on these practices and not buy into them blindly.

To remember that our bodies are the earth is one of the deepest healing practices we can do. We can recognize that each wrinkle is a canyon formed by tears and laughter, joy and sorrow. To reframe our thoughts so that each new growth on our skin is a new mountain, a new hill, a place that increases our worth, not diminishes it. That every stretch mark is a ripple of silvery time etching her way across our bodies as strands of wisdom. Each new lump of cellulite is the soft mound of dimpled sand that one has piled high to see the horizon a bit better. That each new ache and pain is a reminder that our bodies are impermanent and are on a journey back to the earth.

I am thirty-four (at publication) and have yet to experience certain aspects of aging and changes that the body goes through. My older friends talk about how hard it is to accept these changes, especially when they were once beautiful, young women. Yet, I strongly believe if we can turn our minds toward our connection to the mother, to the living earth, we can see how our bodies reflect the earth at every phase in life. When I look at the stretch marks on my thighs, I can choose to be horrified, or I can see how these lines look like the rippling water lines of sunlight across the bottom of the ocean. I know that it is easier said than done, that it is hard to resist standing in front of the mirror and pulling up your face, but I also believe we can do it. We can use the immense love of our own inner Healer to reclaim our true beauty.

EXERCISE 4.1

Lying on Mother Earth

Connecting to our inner Healer helps us to mother ourselves and develop self-love. When the love for our self grows, it fills up our heart and then naturally overflows outward toward others. When we deeply nourish ourselves, we touch the loving quality of motherhood; the expansive, infinite healing part of us. Ammachi, the saint from South India who travels the world giving millions of people a touch of grace through a warm, motherly embrace, says, "The essence of motherhood is not restricted to women who have given birth; it is a principle inherent in both women and men. It is an attitude of the mind. It is love—and that love is the very breath of life…for those in whom motherhood has awakened, love and compassion are as much part of their being as breathing."[10]

---

10.   www.ammachi.org.

To help awaken our inner Healer, we can connect with the earth as a mother and remember that our body is really her body. This is a simple exercise to reconnect you with the earth. Pick a morning or afternoon when you can be alone. Find a place, either in your yard or at a park, where you can lie directly on the earth. Figure out the best way to lie, on your back or side, and do so for some time. Focus on your breath and let your muscles and bones sink into the flesh of the earth. The earth has a pulse too, a rhythm, and by being present you may tap into that pulse, the energetic "breathing" that moves through the planet.

As you lie there, imagine looking at yourself from above. See yourself lying on the grass and slowly move outward to see your body in the park, then the larger city, the state. Let yourself spiral out and up, seeing the state melt into the country, the continent, and finally the entire earth, spinning on its axis, rotating around the sun. Remembering that we are on a planet that is moving thousands of miles every day reminds us that we are constantly in flux, that nothing is permanent.

After some time, slowly drift back down to your continent, country, state, and place where you are lying. Notice that your breath has deepened and you are in a state of complete relaxation. This is a good time to practice a journey, if you are accustomed to it. Journey and meet with your spirit guide and ask for healing and renewal or any other question you may have. When you are finished, slowly sit up and press your hands into the earth. Feel gratitude for being alive, being present with the very being that nourishes and supports your life every day.

Mami Wata

Mami Wata is likely the most worshipped mermaid today and honored as the goddess of water, wealth, healing, and magical powers in Africa, the Caribbean, and the Americas. She is a striking contemporary goddess who works powerful healing magic needed for our aching planet. She has the ability to cross great divides and is one of the most potent images of the sacred feminine. Unbound to any particular place, she swims through many kinds of waters, absorbing, dancing, and reflecting the varied traditions of Africa, India, Santeria, and Latino culture. Mami Wata wanders the waters of the earth as a beautiful, haunting, sumptuous, multicultural, and multidimensional spirit of healing and bounty.

As a mermaid, she is sometimes called an in-betwixter or between creature: part woman, part fish. She appears sometimes black-skinned, other times white, with wild bountiful hair. Trans-gendered, Mami Wata is portrayed as both female and male; she is transcontinental, an African goddess influenced by imagery on European ships from five hundred years ago. She is transmutative, often shown holding snakes, the animal that sheds its skin and is known for its healing symbolism. She is transformative, easily changing shape and her associations, just as water does, to dance with sacred aspects of a myriad of cultures. Mami Wata also shows us the importance of art and its use in both healing and transformation. She is accessible for all women as the powerful Healer archetype.

Mami Wata is both the great mother goddess of primordial life energy, female deity of the sea, as well as mami watas, the smaller watery spirits of various types and kinds that navigate through cultures, as diverse as rivers, waterways, marshes, tributaries, lakes, and ponds. In the Mandé languages of West Africa, both river and mother are the same word, *ba*. Thus Mami Wata is also connected to the more ancient goddess Faro, the spirit of water. According to West African scholar Naomi Doumbia, "Faro arises from her bed in the deep crevices of the river's bottom, visiting us through watery vapor, showering us with rain, streaking the sky with colorful rainbows, communicating to us through thunder, and punishing our infringements of taboos with lightning…Faro represents the word, the word which connects all things; the means by which the world comes to reflect upon and express itself."[11] Some cultures fear her associations with wealth, sexuality, fecundity, wildness, and women, while others worship her and make offerings so they may receive the gift of healing, a child, or magical powers. In the story below, Mami Wata appears a dark and beautiful mermaid, Mama Jo. This tale comes from the southeastern coast of the United States and is retold by Robert D. San Souci; it illustrates how the story of Mami Wata has migrated from one continent to another.

Sukey and the Mermaid[12]

A young girl named Sukey lived in her old, ramshackle cabin on a windy island. She lived out each day a dreary existence under the thumb of her cranky stepfather, Mr. Jones. Sukey secretly nicknamed him "Mr. Hard Times" as he forced her to work all day doing endless chores, hoeing the back garden, washing clothes, cooking meals.

One day, Sukey escaped and ran to sit on the sandy shore next to the sea. The sun was shimmering across the water and the smell of pungent salt filled her nostrils. She breathed deeply, enjoying the quiet solitude away from her troublesome home. As her mind drifted, her gaze settled on the beautiful sea beyond. Sukey felt the cool breeze brush her skin as she pushed her toes into the soft, wet sand. She remembered a song that she had heard once before and sang it aloud:

---

11. Naomi Doumbia, "African Goddess: Mother of Shadow and Light."

12. This story by Robert San Souci is adapted here with his permission from the following source: Robert D. San Souci and Brian Pinkney (illustrator), *Sukey and the Mermaid*. New York: Aladdin Paperbacks, 1992.

Down below the ocean water,
Come and see me, Mama Jo.

Suddenly, a mermaid emerged from the waves! The mermaid was the loveliest thing Sukey had ever seen. She had a beautiful bright face, dark skin, shining black eyes, and wild green hair. She introduced herself to Sukey, "I am Mama Jo." Mama Jo coaxed Sukey out into the cool, fresh waves where they played and frolicked all day long. At the end of the day, Mama Jo gave Sukey a gold coin to take home to her parents.

Sukey was thrilled by her meeting with the mermaid and began to sneak out from her home every day to visit her. Mama Jo became Sukey's friend and taught her how to swim. Each time they met, Mama Jo gave Sukey a gold coin before leaving. Sukey brought the money home to her parents so that she could go play with Mama Jo without having to work. Inevitably, Sukey's mother's suspicions arose as day after day Sukey brought home gold coins. One afternoon, she followed Sukey to the beach and spied on her. There, she saw Sukey playing with the beautiful mermaid and then saw Mama Jo give her the gold coin.

Sukey's mother ran back to the house and told Mr. Jones about the mermaid. They plotted to capture Mama Jo for themselves so they could get more gold. They rowed out to sea and called to Mama Jo, just as Sukey had before:

Down below the ocean water,
Come and see me, Mama Jo.

When Mama Jo surfaced, they tried to capture her with nets, throwing them out into the sea over Mama Jo. But Mama Jo was far too quick for bumbling humans and escaped easily, swimming back into the depths of the ocean.

Sukey, horrified by their attempt to capture her precious friend, ran away to Mama Jo. The beautiful mermaid took Sukey down under the sea to live with her in watery beauty and soft comfort.

At first Sukey adored her new life. She learned many things from Mama Jo about ancient history and the wonderful healing properties of mermaids. But, after awhile, she longed for other humans and begged to return to her home. Reluctantly, Mama Jo brought Sukey back to the beach and gave her a bag of gold to take home. Before Sukey left the sea, Mama Jo told her, "One day, many men will come and ask your hand in marriage, but you must marry only one man. His name is Dembo."

Sukey was welcomed home by her overjoyed mother and mean-hearted stepfather. When Mr. Jones saw the bag of gold, he plotted again to steal it. Sukey was grown up by then and carried the wisdom of dear Mama Jo in her heart. When many men came to court her, she refused them. Finally Dembo appeared. He was a kind and gentle man, full of love for Sukey, and she, in return, fell deeply in love with him. In a fit of rage and terror, Mr. Jones lashed out against Dembo and killed him, stealing the precious bag of gold from Sukey. Sukey screamed in terror at Mr. Jones's vicious act and ran to the sea for help. She called for Mama Jo just as she had as a child:

> Down below the ocean water,
> Come and see me, Mama Jo.

Mama Jo surfaced once again, beautiful and wondrous. Sukey told her of her troubles and pleaded Mama Jo to help her. Mama Jo agreed and gave Sukey a seed pearl that would bring Dembo back to life.

Racing home, Sukey, covered in tears and shaking, placed the pearl in Dembo's mouth. After a few moments, Dembo awoke and they embraced, filled with joy to be reunited. The townspeople, upon hearing of Mr. Jones's dreadful act, chased him into the sea where he was swallowed up by a sudden storm. Sukey and Dembo watched his disappearance into the storm, falling back relieved onto the beach. They found a final gift from Mama Jo, a bag of golden coins that had been buried in the sand, and took each other's hands, happy to be in love, with their small fortune and freed of Mr. Jones.

Keys to the Tale

Sukey is a poor and overworked girl, on the edge of womanhood, who is under the thumb of her stepfather. As a young black girl, Sukey carries the burden of her people and her gender, yet she also contains the gift of a powerful story that has its roots in her distant homeland. Sukey is the young girl in each of us who seeks healing and guidance when dealing with our hard times. Sukey does not need to accomplish anything to receive healing and love, she is simply available. After we have reclaimed our power, we are also ready for deep healing and precious gifts.

Mr. Jones, or, as Sukey calls him, "Mr. Hard Times," is the part of our mind that still seeks to oppress us, that is critical and overbearing. He is the aspect of our lives that prevents us from receiving real nourishment and looks to get in the way of our healing. As women, often we not only have many duties and chores, we also give to others more than giving to ourselves. Sukey reminds us that we too must break away from this part of us and remember that sometimes, "Saying no is actually saying yes." Not only saying no, but also physically removing ourselves from our hectic and fast-paced life is crucial to our own healing. Just as Sukey does, we must choose to escape every once in awhile and seek a nourishing place, like a beach, a retreat center, a walk in the woods. Finding a place in nature is one of the most healing things we can do.

As Sukey rests on the beach, she meets a guide, a magical helper, a wondrous friend. Mama Jo, the beautiful dark-skinned mermaid, loves Sukey completely and unconditionally. This is crucial on our path, knowing that even in times of great aloneness and suffering we have guides around us, healers, helpers, and special spirits who can assist us in our troubles. The mermaid in particular reveals one of the precious qualities of the sacred feminine, the ability to extend healing power through the waters of our earth. The mermaid is the Healer and gives Sukey powers in the form of gold to overcome the obstacles of her own life and navigate through the hardships bearing the wisdom of the Goddess.

Mama Jo is likely connected to the watery mermaid goddess, Mami Wata. Barbara Walker says the image of the mermaid descends from "very old traditions connecting Goddess figures with the sea as a universal womb."[13] We find water spirits and mermaids not only in Africa, but in cultures worldwide. In medieval times, the image of the double fish tailed siren was called a nixie or evil water spirit. Yet, the nixies were more likely daughters of the primordial goddess named Nyx or mother night, who hovered over ancient waters, rather than evil spirits. The nixies were similar to the Greek nereids, female water spirits known to Christian authorities as "she-devils."[14] In India and eastern Asia, the Nagas were similar to mermaids, half human and half water serpents that lived in springs and rivers, guarding treasure. Interestingly, Mami Wata is often portrayed holding snakes, the powerful quality of transformation and healing that is ever-present in goddess symbolism. These images of watery feminine spirits portray the regenerative forces and wisdom of the Healer archetype.

From the first meeting with Mama Jo, Sukey receives a gold coin each day and brings them back to her parents to be exchanged for food. Gold is also a symbol of spiritual wealth and wisdom that Mama Jo is imparting on Sukey. Mama Jo is the Healer who provides both material and spiritual nourishment. Yet, Sukey's mother

---

13.   Barbara Walker, *The Woman's Dictionary of Symbols and Sacred Objects*, p. 263.

14.   Walker, p. 266.

and stepfather become greedy and seek to destroy the mermaid and gain their own wealth, seeing the gold only as material, not the true spiritual wisdom. Sukey's parents are not seeking Mama Jo from the purity of their own hearts, and she escapes back to her home in the water.

Sukey then decides to join Mama Jo, staying with the mermaid in her underwater caves and learning her ways. Similarly, Zimbabwe legends speak of shamanic practitioners who tell the story of visiting the *nsuzu*, or water spirit. This spirit, like Mami Wata, is associated with snakes, rainbows, whirlwinds, and healing. When a medicine person visits with this special water spirit, who lives at the bottom of lakes or rivers, she or he is given powerful healing talents. Sukey also receives a special gift from Mama Jo, a piece of advice she carries in her heart. Mama Jo tells her many men will come for her, but to only choose one in particular, Dembo. She also gives Sukey a large bag of gold this time. Thus Sukey returns bearing the gifts and wisdom of the sea creature and Healer.

When Sukey returns, just as Mama Jo has told her, many men try to court her, but she only falls in love with Dembo. Dembo represents the aspect of us that reflects our inner feminine united with the whole and healed inner masculine. Many parts of us clamor for that recognition, but only the pure and clear-sighted part of us can properly unite our inner masculine and feminine. Still, in that moment, the critical self will often return and lay claim over that pure, healed aspect of our being. Just as our demons may arise again in the glimpse of pure enlightenment, Sukey's own stepfather reacts violently at Sukey's choice, killing Dembo and stealing the gold. When we work toward deep healing, we may reach territory where the old demons try to claw their way to the surface and sabotage our progress. Often when we open ourselves up to the love, we become vulnerable in our surrender and latent fears. The Healer must work a bit harder to overcome these obstacles and remember the power of our guides.

This final violence of Mr. Jones against Dembo also represents the intense push for us to again return to our deep, inner healing resources, just as Sukey returns to Mama Jo for her life-saving pearl. This is the classic pearl of wisdom, the pearl of enlightenment, beauty, purity shining forth from the depths of our watery souls. Mama Jo, the mermaid, carries this wisdom and in great times of need gives it as a life-saving obstacle remover. This wisdom is akin to the stories of African shamans who return from their underwater journeys bearing the ability to heal certain ailments. Sukey's choice to return to the world above also reflects the path of the initiate who has gained deep and transformative healing wisdom and can pass this on to others. This is the true power of the Healer.

In the final scenes of the story, the oppressive Mr. Jones is swallowed up by a storm, a common symbol associated with Mama Jo, mermaids, and African water spirits. This storm is a watery magical power and works to finally dissolve our inner turmoil once and for all, leaving us healed and blessed. Sukey is finally back on the beach where her journey began, sitting with her dear heart, Dembo, counting their precious blessings of gold from Mama Jo. As we begin to heal ourselves, we know that we must channel this healing outward to heal others as well, that indeed we are all connected. The mermaid image of Mama Jo is cruising her way through the waters of the world as a very real spirit of modern times. She is the pure Healer, a living poem and expression of our hearts which, touched by her, can then pass healing on to others.

Dream Healing

Myths are akin to dreams, and by working with world stories we develop a better understanding for symbolism and archetypes. Our inner Healer has a strong connection to alternative realities and can be called on for working with our dreams. Occasionally we have a healing or initiatory dream that gives us powerful insight into the deeper parts of ourselves on the path of spirit. These dreams are special, and we can return to them to find continued insight as we navigate through our lives. They often give us clues as to what we need to embrace or heal, or act as the healing themselves. In the case of my dream below, it firstly helped me to reconcile our return to India, which I had been feeling very doubtful about. Any kind of initiatory dream is also a reminder that we are not alone, that spirit and helpers are guiding us at all times.

A Personal Healing Dream

I am walking along the narrow, dusty-red back roads of Varkala, Kerala in South India (where my home was at the time). Brilliant vermillion hibiscus and vivid fuchsia bougainvillea bob their luscious heads in the dappled sunlight, hanging loose and relaxed over whitewashed walls like the women who rest their elbows, smiling in the late afternoon light, dark eyes shining, hair oiled with coconut and decorated with jasmine. They are drinking chai and calling, "Hallo…sugam danay!" I am walking slowly, carefully, under the coconut trees that rustle in the luscious breeze. The feel of it on my skin makes me so alive, so full of breath and light and wind. Ahead of me is a cement wall with a new gate that has yet to be whitewashed. Someone has painted childish stars and hearts on the wall.

I want to go inside, through the gate, but suddenly a woman is there and she is giving birth. This is the second baby of twins, and she has just delivered the other a few hours before, in a nearby house. I am there to catch the baby, to midwife it into the world. He comes out, dark and gorgeous, into my open arms as easy as a coconut dropping from a tree. His eyes are full of love and radiance; he is covered in blood, a pure, brilliant, magickal blood, the life force of the universe. I press him close to me and feel so full of joy and wonder. As I hold him close, he begins to grow and grow. He expands outward and upward, and my spirit fills with even more light and love. Then he is a tall being, much taller than me, with a kind of colorful mask on his face or an energy pattern. Suddenly we are surrounded by eleven more of these beings, all with these colorful masks, each one completely unique. They number twelve altogether. They seem to each represent a different energy of the universe. I feel so honored to be in the middle of this circle as they send their love and tell me, in my mind, this is an initiation.

I woke suddenly, in the middle of the night, and realized I was not in Varkala, but at my parents' home in Maryland. My seven-month-old infant was lying next to me, her mouth slightly open, a film of breast milk around it. I was full of brightness and awe as I remembered the dream, knowing it was a powerful one, one to remember. My dear friend had given me a tarot reading with her Ancestral Tarot deck the night before and I pulled the Initiation card. This was obviously a direct connection to the dream, the dream of initiation. We returned to Varkala a few months later, and I walked down that very lane where the dream took place. I later felt these beings were akin to the Orishas and this is what may have initiated me that night, or something very similar. These beings in their various guises such as the Orishas, the Kachina, or the Oracle are guiding forces who initiate people into the magical powers of life.

Keys to the Dream

This was a healing dream that I felt was both preparing me for my return to India and foretelling parts of that season in India, which in the months following brought me even more in touch with Africa, of all things. I taught Reiki that season to a dear friend who is Senegalese and his wife who has studied African mythology extensively. In some West African cultures, twins carry special messages from the spirit world. According to West African healer and scholar Ken and Naomi Doumbia, "Twins are the children of the spirit of water, Faro—the spirit who reflects, like a mirror, the shadow or double of creation."[15] Interestingly, the second-born twin is believed to be the eldest, having sent the first one to check out the situation. In my dream, I delivered the second twin.

As the dream continued, I received the boy child, covered in the primordial, life-giving blood. This blood is pure magic in my dream: it glows and sparkles and fills me with joy and brilliance. Birth blood, easily dismissed as disgusting, unattractive, or filthy, was traditionally believed to hold woman's power as she gave her blood to bring new life into the world. Acting as the midwife for the birth, I received the power of this blood, which in ancient times, in a myriad of cultures, was considered the magical substance that creates life. Menstruation blood, which is held in during the creation of children, is akin to the cycles of the moon and attributed great power in a multitude of myths and stories. Countless creation stories speak of humans born of the Great Mother from the magical bloody flow of sacred feminine consciousness. Celtic kings became gods when they drank the menses blood of the goddess; girls are still prized in some African cultures because they have the powerful moon bloods; South American indigenous people believe that the first humans were made of moon blood.

Finally, in my dream, the newborn boy, embraced in my arms, grows into a mystical being. The feeling during that part of the dream was utterly magical; I was suffused with an overwhelming feeling of joy and love. As he grew taller and taller, his face turned into a kind of masked being or spirit that loomed over me, blessing

---

15. Adama and Naomi Doumbia, *The Way of the Elders*, p. 120.

me. Suddenly I was surrounded by spirit beings who proceeded to send me a bolt of energy that I was told was an initiation. They all had unique characteristics and were certainly a kind of tribe unto themselves, a group that blessed me with the power of love and healing.

For years I have reflected back on this dream, using it as a tool for transformation, love, and power. I felt I was seeded with certain qualities from the dream that I am slowly learning about as my life unfolds. I have received very few dreams such as this one; with such vibrancy, brilliance and a feeling of incredible joy.

EXERCISE 4.2

Journaling a Dream

Think of a dream that had a powerful impact on you. It should be one that you clearly remember, one that was vivid in color, felt wonderful or beautiful, or perhaps was frightening. This should be a dream that you have held close to your heart for many years. If you cannot think of a dream, then use a story that you love or that your mind often returns to. Write it down as a fairy tale and try to look at it with fresh eyes. How is the dream still benefiting you today? What insight can you gain from the dream? How can you more fully integrate the lessons given to you from your healing dream? Even if the dream was many years ago, it still holds a potent power in your life. This is because our spiritual selves do not work in linear time. Although our bodies decay from birth to death, we are vast, multidimensional beings that are actually operating in different dimensions; we have simply forgotten. Healing dreams help us to remember.

Water Ceremony

This ritual is a ceremony to honor the water on our planet, on mother earth and in our bodies, as well as a rite of healing and cleansing. This ceremony activates the loving Healer within. Many people who vacation at the beach are seeking out water as a healing balm. In the Zulu language of Africa, *icibi* means lake and *icibella* means "to patch." This is because the lake literally patches up the environment, by absorbing toxins and cleansing them. Peoples around the world give offerings and perform ceremonies in water in a myriad of ways. In India, they put the ashes of their departed back "home" in the waters, and in Brazil they honor Yemaya, goddess of the waters, on February 2, giving offerings of fruits and flowers to the ocean.

The best place to do this ritual is at a body of water, at the ocean or a lake, by a spring, next to a river or stream, or even at a well. If it is impossible to make a ritual at such a place, then you can simply fill a large bowl of water and use that, although I do recommend that you find a natural water source, as there are elementals that support and guide your practice. Elementals are spirits of a place and/or an element (water, air, fire, and earth) that protect the energy of that place and work in harmony with the earth. A potent time to start this ceremony is just before sunrise or sunset, so that the transition into day or night happens during the ritual—a transition which in itself is rarely given our complete attention.

The best time to do a healing water ritual is during the waxing or full moon. The full moon is especially beautiful if you can visit the water source at night, as the moonlight reflecting on the water brings more power to the space. This ceremony can be combined with giving offerings to the ancestors and/or a full moon ritual. It can be very simple and quiet, or longer with a lot of music and song; it can be done alone or in a group. Gather together what you will need for your ceremony: a blue or silver silken cloth (or any cloth you can use as an altar on the ground); offerings for the four cardinal directions; an oil lamp (if possible, although this is not necessary; this consists of a small clay or ceramic shallow bowl, a string wick, and a bit of oil to keep the fire burning—unlike candles, it will not blow out); incense; rattles and other sound makers; small boats to float offerings such as coconut shells, pieces of wood, or large leaves; small offerings such as tiny stones, sand, fruit, or bits of ash for the boat; a large bag full of flower petals such as roses, daisies, bougainvillea, or if it is fall or winter, you can use leaves and berries; several small bowls; water brought from your home.

If your spot is at a public place, such as in a park or a public beach, find an area that is farthest away from people. If you are in a group, you may need to be mindful of how your presence will affect those around you. This ceremony can be done gently and quietly without attracting too much attention; however, if you can find a secluded spot, all the better. You may use your small oil lamp or build a fire, depending on where you are. Set up the space with your ceremonial items by first laying down the cloth, then putting your offerings in each of the four directions. Pile your offerings of flower petals and/or gathered plant pieces in the center of the cloth. Light the incense and oil lamp or make a fire. Then create your sacred space, giving offerings of water from your home to the seven directions to honor the elementals of the place.

After calling the directions, honoring earth, sky, and center, then sit quietly and listen deeply to the sounds of the place: the trickle of the stream, the crash of the waves, the quiet lapping of lake ripples, or the echo of water dripping into the well. Spend at least twenty minutes sitting in silence, quietly allowing the sound, the smell, the vision of the water to fill up your senses, your being. Close your eyes after some time and feel the air on your skin and continue listening to the sounds, allowing yourself to merge with the water. Visualize your heart opening to the others in the circle and to the water. If you feel a desire to call a goddess of the water, you may choose Yemaya, Oshun, Mami Wata, or Aphrodite. You may wish to call the power of the water itself, or any water spirit you feel a connection with, or simply the energy of water to bless you. Focus on your breath for several moments once you have done this, then get up and fill one of the small bowls with water from the water source. Add some of your water from your house, saying, "Water spirits, may you bless this water, this melding of place and self, breath and spirit." Then sprinkle the water on yourself and all the others present. Sprinkle the water on the altar as well, on the objects there and the flower petals. Visualize yourself as the Healer, casting healing waters on each person.

Then sing a song that you feel connects you to water. You may choose to use your sound makers now, rattling and soft drumming as appropriate for the space. Sing for some time, allowing your voices to rise and fall like the water, finding their own rhythm. If you feel uncomfortable singing, then spend time free toning, simply allowing your voice to open to sound coming through it. Imagine your voice as a gift to the water and earth.

After some time, the singing will begin to slow, then end. Again spend time in quiet space, watching as the night turns to day or the day to night, listening to the change in sounds that accompany the earth turning. Then have everyone gather their small "boat" of wood or coconut along with many flower petals and bring them to the water side. As you sit by the water, place an offering on your boat to float on the water. It can be very simple, such as a few petals, or more elaborate with incense and an oil lamp even, if it is okay to float this. One of the most beautiful images is a small flame on water and can evoke a sense of awe.

This is a deliberate and specific offering to the water spirit herself. You are giving a gift of healing to the waters of the earth. Contemplate the power and beauty of water as you construct your small boat using what you have gathered before the ceremony. This is an act of deep gratitude, a gift to the water and thanks for the nourishment it feeds you. Float your boats out into the water, perhaps singing or chanting a song.

After floating the small offerings, gather your flower petals into your lap. These you will also float into the water to ask for healing. You may begin with yourself, but then offer petals to the people you know who need healing, including both people you love and people you dislike. Offer petals for places on earth that need help, countries, environments, lands and waters, governments that will benefit from the healing power of water. Again, take your time and do this for a while, singing or chanting as you feel to. If you are leading this ceremony, you may want to use a soft rattle to accompany this process of healing. Watch as the flower petals take to the current and visualize them drifting to those who will benefit your healing work. When you are finished, return to the altar space and close the sacred circle. You may wish then to share the water you brought from home, or perhaps some food you brought with you. It is also a nice time to just sit with each other after the ritual, admiring the water and connecting through sharing what you have experienced. When you have done ceremony at a particular place by the water, you form a connection to this place and carry it with you in your heart. You can visualize going back there when you do rituals at home, with the power of the water assisting your magical work.

FIVE

THE CONSORT
The Loving Dance

*Become loving. When you are in the embrace,
become the embrace. Become the kiss.
Forget yourself so totally that you can say,
"I am no more. Only love exists."*
—OSHO

*Imagine yourself climbing out of the water and onto a large
flat rock. Comb out your hair and look around you. This is
a completely safe and sacred space. You feel relaxed, enjoying the surroundings with all of your senses. Smell the jasmine, roses, and plumeria that surround you; feel the soft
brush of the breeze on your skin; absorb the heat from the
rock deep into your muscles and bones. Open your heart to
the loving presences of the trees, flowers, and water. Perhaps
you see certain animals, birds, or guides come to your sacred
garden and honor you with their love. You feel incredibly
harmonious with all that surrounds you. As your inner love
grows, you allow it to flow from you and surround you with*

golden light. Visualize a being of intense love lying next to
you on the rock, holding your hand. This being lets energy
flow into you, a safe and sacred liquid stream of light. Feel
the bliss emanating from the guide or friend into your body.
Allow yourself to experience the vital life energy, the orgias-
tic expression of fruitfulness, flowering and growing as you
open even more deeply to inner love.

As we heal, we open more deeply to our loving selves reflected as the Consort, who is a lover or sensual-spiritual partner. The inner Consort is the lover within us, the one who relates to the people in our lives—and not just our partners, husbands, or lovers, but also our children, our parents, our family, and our friends. When our inner Consort is based on a foundation of power, we move through life relating to others with more ease and joy. This also allows us to experience states of loving that emanate from within rather than looking outward to satisfy desires or create happiness. The Consort comes to us in the form of Radha, the Indian lover of Krishna who is completely devoted to him yet also realizes that even when he is gone, they are inseparable, just as our own deep abiding peaceful-ness and self-love is always within, even when masked by pain or sorrow.

The Consort is the unification of our inner masculine and feminine selves, the harmony of opposites that dance the world into being and create beauty, love, and joy. This is the part of us that eventually transcends even those opposites and is a spiritual crea-ture that is able to transmute desire into powerful levels of love and healing. The Consort is like a dancer, flowing with life in a way that is effortless and joyous. This is the movement between opposites, between light and shadow, birth and death, male and female, outer and inner. Exploring and working with the inner love of the self is a potent key to discovering our true being.

The Consort is also the aspect of us that is playful, sexual, and delights in the world of senses. When we stop to smell and purchase flowers for our room, put on lavender or jasmine perfume, delight in beautiful fabrics or the feel of nice sheets, we are experiencing our inner Consort. I encourage you to explore these sensual connections with your outer world as a way to nourish the self. Sometimes we become too busy to stop and smell the roses, but these are the things that imbue life with beauty and quality. Being able to make a space habitable, create a feeling or a mood, design a natural and spontaneous altar out of clutter, choose clothing for a concert that reflects the beauty and power of the music makers—all these are all innate within us and enhance our loving self as we explore the Consort.

Reclaiming the Sexual-Spiritual

The sensual energy that burns within women has been coerced into a very small space, and at times dominated completely. As with the Warrioress, there is a measure of fear associated with the sexual power that resides within women. Sexual-spiritual problems are buried within all of us, after experiencing generations of abuse and distortion. Today, one in three women is abused at some point in her life; one in five is raped. So when we begin to work with our inner Consort, there is a chance we are opening up a can of worms. The sexual energy of our being is often overwhelmingly separated from our notion of the spiritual. I see us on a stepping stone between two systems, one that does not honor the sacred feminine and one that does. Devanayagi Parameswaran, a Tantric teacher and sacred feminine leader, captures well the importance of healing this issue, saying, "When women are in their power, everyone in the world benefits. The entire universe is a dance between polarities, deified as Shiva and Shakti. To live a happy and healthy existence we must learn how to bring love and enjoyment into the dance we call relationships. Men must learn to nurture women so women may reclaim and maintain their divine powers. Women must redefine their expression of power to salvage the future of the Next Generation."[16]

Our society is currently exploring the deeper possibilities of sexual energy, finding that women can have multiple orgasms extended over a long period of time. Women (and men) are capable of not just genital orgasm but orgasmic states that move through the entire body. Indeed, we are all born directly of this powerful creative life energy and by engaging in sexuality we are tapping into that power. This power is not only limited to pleasure; it is useful for healing, setting intentions, creating new projects, worlds, and ideas. I was pleased to read in Vicki Noble's *Shakti Woman* how she rubs her legs together, bringing herself to orgasm, which helps her concentrate on various things, including her studies. I too have used this energy while studying for exams, writing, creating art. I use the energy that rises up as a way to imbue healing, prayers, and intentions into my work, so that they are further suffused with the life force. It is easy to dismiss this action as weird or aberrant, but in reality it is simply the life force, and we have for too long been disconnected from this healing energy. If we just look around us, we see the whole earth is in the process of making life, making love, rubbing, pollinating, birthing, and growing. Spirituality is sexuality in its true sense, the loving consciousness of self, the earth, and each other.

Also crucial to this process is the development and nurturance of the healthy masculine, the reclaiming of men who can be soft and receptive as well as skillful and imbued with their own inner

---

16. Devanayagi Parameswaran, "Tantra: From Om to Orgasm," www.humanityhealing .ning.com.

power, love, and wisdom. Time and again, through the process of researching and writing this book, I have come across intensely condescending and hurtful words toward God, the god, the male, and the masculine. At times it even goes so far as to condemn the patriarchal system in a way that also condemns anything male. I understand, as a woman reading about the mass domination and the centuries of suppression, how much rage and fury is there and needs to be honored and that we are still entrenched in a system that is a kind of dominator culture that objectifies women. Yet, we can work to transcend these ideas; we do not have to fixate on our gender, but can allow this to loosen and dissolve a little, to recognize instead the dance between men and women, between male and female, between black and white, between negative and positive. We honor the incredible dance between birth and death, growth and decay, transcendence and groundedness. Working to more completely embrace the sacred feminine allows us to honor the sacred masculine as well, to redefine what that means in our lives, as well as in the lives of men around us. The inner Consort is the quality of that dance between the sacred feminine and masculine and developing our love so that it enriches our life more fully.

EXERCISE 5.1

Raising Energy

The first step in working with the loving sensuality of the Consort is to get in touch with your own vital life force and reconnect it with your entire life, instead of limiting it to sexual relationships. By doing this, you will help further heal your sacred feminine so that it empowers you with sensual self-love, enhances your energy, and boosts your vital life force. Many, many women associate their inner happiness with an external source, particularly finding a partner or man. Of course, this is a wonderful part of life, being with a partner, perhaps creating a family and connecting with community; however, it is even more important to recognize your own vital sexual energy and practice inner love so that you don't rely on other people to fill that need for you. Once you find your own inner resources, the kinds of loving relationships you desire will find you more naturally.

This is a simple exercise to practice using your sexual energy in ways that are not related to normal sexual activity. First, choose something that you want to heal or manifest in your life. This could be anything from healing a bad relationship to manifesting a new car. Clearly visualize what you want to heal or manifest. If it is a healing, imagine the issue or health problem as healthy and use the sexual energy to vitalize the life force. Next, use self-pleasuring to stimulate your energy so that you move into a heightened state of intense feeling. If you are unaccustomed to practicing self-pleasure, then just touch your body in a way that feels good, natural, and easeful. Remember this is a practice to use sexual energy for your life, to enhance the beauty of life, rather than having a sexual fantasy. In this way you are reclaiming the connections between sensual energy and life. As you self-pleasure, if you are able to reach orgasm, then do so, and continue visualizing what you want to heal or manifest. Imagine the image radiating with waves of loving energy, radiating out into the surrounding environment.

As you come down from your orgasm, or feel ready to end the practice, then simply rest, pressing your hands to your heart. Breathe into the beauty of your body, of sensual pleasure and open-heartedness. If you feel pain, guilt, or shame while doing this practice, then send love to that area of your being. If this practice is really an issue and you are afraid or have no experience with self-pleasure, you may want to seek out further guidance to help heal the issues that are preventing you from accessing your vital life forces. In Chapter Two, Exercise 2.2 can help you reclaim the power and love that you deserve as a sensual and sexual being on earth. Just as you did with your reclaiming initiation, you can use this to reclaim your rightful sexual self. If further trauma arises, such as issues with abuse, I would recommend seeking out a healer or therapist who can further support deeper work.

Tantra

For thousands of years, most religious dogma has systematically split the two most powerful energies available to us: the spiritual and the sexual. We have been doggedly told generation after generation that the way to heaven, to God, to paradise is found through transcendence and letting go of the material, sexual, birthing body. Since the beginning of that split, perhaps some 6,000 years ago, only a few remains are left of the goddess worshiping culture, which unites the spiritual and sexual. One of those remains is Tantra, which literally means "web" and "to expand." Tantric philosophy became prominent in India around 1,500 years ago in the fourth and fifth centuries. In historical terms, this is actually quite recent and marks one of the most accessible practices of honoring the sacred feminine in human religious history. Long before this, it is thought that Tantra was practiced by the goddess worshipping society of Dravidian people before being conquered by the Aryans circa 3000 BCE. According to Sjöö and Mor, it was likely that "in ancient times the special potency of Tantra was transmitted through a female line of 'power-holders'—a mysterious sect of women called the Vratyas."[17]

In Tantra, women are the focus of the ancient yogic tradition. Swami Muktananda, an advanced yogic practitioner, in her discourse on female yoga states, "In the tantric tradition, the woman is considered to be higher than the man so far as the tantric initiations are concerned...[this] is purely a spiritual attitude in relation

17. Sjöö and Mor, p. 219.

to the evolution of higher consciousness. The frame of a woman, her emotions, and her psychic evolution is definitely higher than that of a man. Awakening of the spiritual force (kundalini) is much easier in the body of a woman than in the body of a man."[18] This is a profound and compelling statement. She goes on to explain that because of the way our bodies cycle each month and are made for birth we have a higher capacity to connect to the spiritual world. Our sexuality is a reflection of this connection. Psychic dreams, visioning, journeying, and traveling between the worlds are as natural to women as menstruation and birth.

Krishna and Radha

Hindu mythology explores Tantra through the sensuous beauty of the lovers Krishna and Radha. Krishna is the loving and compassionate god, holding the qualities of beauty and making gorgeous music with his flute. He is blue, the color of peace and serenity, and is often painted or figured in a dancing pose, on the verge of joyous movement. Many images of Krishna include his loving partner Radha, and they gaze into each other's eyes, hands meeting, with sensuous clothing and beautiful colors adorning their bodies and surroundings. They are the archetypal lovers as well as symbols of our inner male and female, the beauty of the inner Consort that finds the balance of joy and loving within.

The Tale of Krishna and Radha[19]
One lovely day, Nanda the cow herder went to Vrindavan, carrying his tiny infant son Krishna. He brought his cattle to graze by the banyan tree in the grove. Krishna, a bit bored, began to cast clouds

---

18. Swami Muktananda, *Nawa Yogini Tantra*, p. 4.

19. Dimmitt, Cornelia, and J. A. B. van Buitenen. *Classical Hindu Mythology: A Reader in the Sanskrit Puranas*. Philadelphia: Temple University Press, 1978.

in the sky, creating a coming storm. The sound of thunder rumbled far off and the clouds grew darker as the trees shook violently in the winds. Krishna began to cry and clung to his father, afraid of his own creation.

In the middle of this wild storm, the beautiful woman Radha appeared, emerging out of the pouring rains. She slowly walked toward Nanda and Krishna, swaying gently like swans. Radha's eyes reminded Nanda of lotuses, and the darkness around them made them glow. Just between her eyes shone a large, beautiful pearl. Jasmine flowers dripped down her long, thick black braid and their fragrance filled the air. When Nanda saw her, he could not move, as her beauty was more great and wondrous than the light of many moons. Suddenly, tears sprung to his eyes and he bowed deeply, his heart opened in great devotion, and he offered her his child, Krishna. The illustrious Radha took the child, laughing delightedly. Radha offered Nanda a wish for anything he might like, but Nanda wanted only to remain in servitude to Radha. She happily granted Nanda unsurpassed servitude and love.

Radha then clutched Krishna to her heart and took him far away, embracing and kissing him as he began to remember the circle of their dance, quivering in joy. As she twirled around, forgetting herself in the dance of love, Krishna turned into a lovely handsome youth. He had warm dark skin, and smelled of sweet sandalwood. He lay down on a bed of flowers, smiling at Radha, so beautiful and serene, his eyes peaceful and full of love.

Seeing that the infant had changed into this glowing youth who lay before her, Radha was dazzled by his handsome body and her eyes drank the moonlight off his face. Eager for a new union and shivering over her entire body, she smiled, completely smitten with love. He said to her, "Radha, you are dearer to me than my own life. As am I, so are you, and there is no difference between us. Just as there is whiteness in milk, and heat in fire, and fragrance in earth, so am I in you always. A potter cannot make a pot without clay, nor a goldsmith an earring without gold. Likewise I cannot create without you, for you are the soil of creation and I am the seed. You are the woman, I am the man."

Radha and Krishna were married by the god Brahma, the Lotus-Born One. They performed the marriage thread ceremony and circumambulated the fire seven times. Radha recited three mantras and placed a garland of parijata blossoms around Krishna's neck. Krishna placed a lovely garland around Radha's neck and then sat beside Brahma. They brought their hands together in prayer position at the heart center, and Brahma gave Radha to Krishna, as the father gives away his daughter.

Alone with Krishna, Radha was made shy and bashful by the intensity of their love. Shivering in excitement, Radha adorned Krishna with beautiful scents of aloe, sandal, musk, and saffron. She handed him a jewel encrusted cup filled with nectar and honey. He drank deeply from it, savoring the sweet flavors that swirled on his tongue. Krishna placed betel nut on Radha's tongue and watched as she enjoyed chewing it in front of him. When he asked her for it, she laughed and refused to give it to him. Krishna then gently rubbed an ointment of sandal, aloe, musk, and saffron all over her limbs under her clothes, then pulled her close to him, against his chest. He loosened her clothing then and kissed her four different ways. The little bell she wore came off and the red lip color spread out over her face from his kisses. Her braid came undone and the vermillion bindi dot fell from her forehead.

Radha's body was completely thrilled by the new union, and she was so dazed and full of love that she had no sense of day or night. Krishna embraced her limb for limb, body for body, playing out the eight ways of love as master of the Kama Sutra. Her body grew tender and sore from his loving bites, while her bracelets and anklets tinkled in their love play. Radha then forced his flute from his hand and Krishna took the mirror from her hand.

When the intense love play was finally over, Radha, smiling and glancing sideways at her beloved, affectionately gave Krishna back his flute and he returned her mirror. He then lovingly re-plaited her braid and carefully put on her vermillion dot. He dressed her with artful skill, paying careful attention to each fold in her clothing, smoothing it beautifully.

When Radha turned to dress Krishna, she found that he shed his youth suddenly and had become an infant once again, crying and hungry, just as Nanda had given him to her. Radha's heart grew heavy and forlorn, and she sighed at the pain of their sudden separation. She fell to the ground sobbing, her heart breaking. That moment, a disembodied voice said, "Why do you weep, Radha? Remember Krishna's dancing lotus feet! As long as the dance exists, he will return to it and you shall have all the love play with Krishna. There is no reason to cry. Take the infant home and know that he will return in due time." Radha was comforted; she took the child but not without glancing once more at the pavilion and flower garden.

Quickly Radha left Vrindavan and went to Nanda's house. She went in the blink of an eye, her lovely dress sticky and wet, and her eyes reddened. She gave the baby over to Krishna's mother, Yasoda, saying, "Your husband was caught by the rain with your child and he is hungry. I had much trouble on the way—my clothes are wet, it's a dreadful rainy day, and I was barely able to carry him on the slippery, muddy road. Take your child, give him the breast and calm him down. I must go now." Yasoda took the infant and kissed him and fed him from her breast, and Radha went home to do her household chores. But every night Krishna returned to her to make love once more.

Keys to the Tale

Out of the wild storm created by Krishna emerges Radha, beautiful and glorious, gentle, like the calm in the center of the storm.

She is not affected by its power or afraid, but is tranquil and glow-ing. Like many goddesses in myths, she possesses a rare beauty, one that shimmers over her entire body, making her glow. This beauty reminds us to embody the Consort within, the one who dances effortlessly and enables us to be at home in our body, honor it, nur-ture it, listen to it, and delight in its sensuality.

Once Nanda recognizes Radha's divinity, he takes refuge in her, seeking her blessing. This portrays the art of surrender that is potent in the loving wisdom of the Consort. Surrendering in love, in lovemaking, in meditation, in life—this is the way toward openness, the path of the heart. When we devote ourselves to cultivating our path and really working with developing ourselves, we are opening the gateway to inner love and resources. Nanda represents the part of us that is the pure, whole-hearted caregiver. In the story, instead of wishing for riches or fame, Nanda wishes simply to devote him-self to Radha as his teacher, and the goddess happily granted Nanda "unsurpassed servitude and love." This may seem strange to us, to wish for the opportunity to serve in pure love, but it is the most potent wisdom of the heart, the purest form of being, and dis-solves the ego completely. I had a similar experience when I met my teacher, an overwhelming wish to simply lie down at his feet and become his rug, forever. This feeling arose naturally after some years of my own work in meditation, Reiki, and contemplative study to help grind down my own self-cherishing. When we surrender to a teaching, a teacher, or a path, we are committed to finding the vast love that resides within.

Krishna then greets Radha with such love, remarking that "Just as there is whiteness in milk, and heat in fire, and fragrance in earth, so am I in you always." This is a powerful message. These quali-ties define the substance; they are the very *essence* of milk, fire, and earth. This illuminates that the two beings are not opposites, as we tend to think of male and female in the West, but are essentially part of each other. The opposite of milk is not white, nor is the opposite of fire heat. They are the very essence of these things, the sensory qualities that make them what they are. Similarly, Krishna compares their relationship to the clay and the potter, the gold and the goldsmith, remarking that a goldsmith cannot be such without gold. Our inner love then is not separate from us; our joy and brilliance are there, they are not at odds with our depression or problems, but simply the essence of who we are as human beings. Activating our inner Consort enables us to reclaim that joy more fully.

Radha and Krishna then perform the wedding ceremony, to spiritually unite one another in sacred marriage. A tantrika, or practitioner of Tantra, may choose to be a householder and practice achieving divine ecstasy through sacred sexuality as well as other meditative and contemplative practices. Muktananda offers her profound wisdom here, noting that "In India a woman traditionally loves and reveres her husband as her guru, and he loves and reveres her as devi, as a goddess. This does not mean that one or the other is spiritually superior, but that the act of loving is the means to transformation, and that the purpose of marriage is to help one another to become greater than we could be alone."[20] This is a complex issue, because in the West, we do not really use marriage as a sadhana, or spiritual practice. Usually, we fall in love and try to maintain a romantic quality in the relationship; when this wears thin, we fall out of love and seek fulfillment elsewhere. When we fall in love, we tend to enhance the positive qualities of our lover, in a semi-delusion that is usually compounded by intense physical attraction. Later, when we discover those qualities to be minimal, we may start to dislike or even resent our lover. This is when we may choose to use our marriage as a sadhana, instead of running out to find a new lover. I am not saying we should stay with someone if we feel unfulfilled, sabotaged, or completely estranged, but I am calling for a closer examination of what our true motivations

---

20. Muktananda, p. 79.

are when we decide to dissolve a relationship. Try devoting yourself to your partner for an entire day, just as Krishna does to Radha, and Radha to Krishna. Listen closely when he or she is speaking to you; instead of getting upset over requested tasks or ideas, simply do them or agree wholeheartedly. Imagine your partner is a teacher you admire and you are spending the day honoring and serving this person instead of taking them for granted. This is something we can strive to do with all the people in our lives, to honor them as aspects of god and goddess. This can be difficult and challenging, as our personal, smaller self will be confronted with the reality that it is less important than the devotional service. Yet this kind of service really encourages our heart to open and our personal attachments to dissolve.

The next part of the myth involves the love play and love-making of Radha and Krishna. After they are blessed by Brahma, their intimacy grows. At first they are gentle and adorn each other with sandal, aloe, musk, and saffron. That in itself is so beautiful, so delightful. Adding elements of sweet-smelling substances and soft oils enhances the sexual experience. This is also a way to tune into your partner, to pay attention to the entire body, not just the genitals. Lovemaking can be a sacred dance, an exploration, an adventure, not just a buildup to physical release. They take off each other's clothing, and the red on her lips spreads out across her face from the kisses. Radha is so enthralled that she has no sense of day or night. She completely loses herself to the new union—which is new in these bodies, yet ancient as well.

The love play, the Tantric dance, is a story of both the outer and inner aspects of ourselves, the outer being our physical and emotional relation to ourselves, our lovers, husbands, partners, and friends. The inner is the inner masculine meeting the inner feminine: both as meditative then as spiritual practice. In the story, in the final sentences describing their lovemaking, they take each other's specific tools or qualities; she takes his flute, he takes her mirror.

They are filling each other up with the other—the masculine filling himself up with the feminine and in turn, the feminine taking on the masculine. Yet even more transcendent is the coming together as one, the deep and utter realization that inner awareness creates the true alchemy of transformation.

In the final passages of the story, to Radha's surprise and sorrow, Krishna retakes the form of an infant, becoming the baby that he was in the beginning of the story. Radha symbolizes the part of us that separates once again from our lover, from that deep inner source of joy; the very real, relentless quality of being alive and having to survive and deal with day-to-day life. It is as if Radha, recognizing her own true nature, her own deep bliss, her own wondrous divinity, is then suddenly separated from this, and not only separated but *conscious* of this separation. She is well aware of the inability to reconnect, for now, with Krishna in that divine way as long as he remains in his baby form. Yet the divine reassures her that he will always return; thus our connection to the divine will also return.

Krishna's return to infant state is a reminder for us to be vulnerable with our lovers, our families, ourselves. Part of this is the dynamic of taking care of each other in relationships; inevitably we all play out the roles of mother, father, child, and sibling. Again we see service and devotedness coming into play. In our society, elders and children are not as valuable as youthful attractive adults and can be brushed aside in the pursuit of money and beauty. This is not useful when we must deal with our partner's or family's aging, sickness, and vulnerability. Just as Radha does, we should allow ourselves to feel into and mourn the changes that happen when the children grow up and leave home, our partner dies, or we fall ill and cannot do some of the things we once did together. Mourning is a process of deep acceptance and helps to soothe our being and nourish inner love.

The final sentence of the myth reminds again of how connected these two are as each and every night Krishna still comes to visit her. Even though they are physically separate, they are still joined in the dreamtime or energetically. Similarly, we are continuously connected to our own inner joy and can access it through meditation, ceremony, myth, and dreams even in times of sorrow or pain.

EXERCISE 5.2

Connecting to Your Inner Masculine

This exercise encourages you to open up to your sacred masculine. Up to this point in the book, we have been working deeply with the sacred feminine and her power and love. We must address the qualities of the god as well as the goddess to achieve a balanced and loving self. Carl Jung, the founder of analytical psychology, spent a good deal of his life working with archetypes, the collective unconscious, and dream imagery. Part of his work addressed the animus or inner opposite self that exists within each of us. Defining our inner masculine helps to feel a sense of balance in our lives and also reduces the overt associations that our culture places on feminine and masculine.

For this exercise, you will need a piece of paper, a pen, and art supplies. Imagine that an inner masculine self resides within you and construct a dialogue with him. Ask him what qualities you associate with masculine and male. Write these down. What qualities or energies would you like to cultivate more fully in your own life, perhaps qualities that are attributed more to men or the realm of the masculine? Which qualities do you feel are also connected to your inner feminine or sacred female? Explore the different aspects of men you know and admire. When are men most appealing to you and why? If you feel negative qualities surfacing regarding the inner male, then send healing light to this part of you. Then use your art supplies to draw your animus or inner masculine. Spend time creating an image of your personal animus, one that speaks to you of sacred masculine qualities.

Finally, imagine the men you know more fully embodying empowering masculine qualities: aspects of courage, fearlessness, honor, and respect that are so needed in our world. Imagine sending love and strength to the healing of the sacred masculine.

Full Moon Ceremony

This ritual is a beautiful way to draw healing power into your body and spirit, as well as energizing and renewing your well-being. A drawing-down-the-moon ceremony can be used for a specific intention such as healing, enhancing intentions, or creating abundance. In this case, we will focus on drawing the moon down into us as sacred power to activate our inner Consort. The full moon is also connected to the mother aspect of the goddess, the ancient symbol of a full, pregnant woman, ripe with life and abundance, joy and well-being. We call on this full moon energy to enhance our own being through the power of ceremony. This ceremony can be done alone or in a group with just women or both men and women. If done in a group, designate specific roles for calling in each of the directions and one women to act as the priestess. The priestess (or yourself if you perform this alone) takes the role of keeping the ritual moving though its different aspects as well as channeling the goddess into drawing down the moon into each participant. This is the key element to the entire ceremony, and the priestess should feel comfortable in her role.

Gather together the following items:

+ Four candles for the four directions, two for mother earth and father sky, plus additional candles or oil lamps to surround you
+ Sensual offerings for the four directions: incense for the east, a rose candle for the south, crystal bowl of water with rose petals for the west, and saffron/sandalwood paste for the north

- Offerings for mother earth (sage, pearls, and/or shells) and father sky (crystals, fairy dust/glitter, and/or feathers)
- Pictures and images that speak to you of abundance, healing, sexual openness
- Symbols of beauty, love, and abundance such as eggs, crystals, feathers, shells, nests, bells
- Rose, sandalwood, lavender, musk, and/or jasmine oil
- Flowers
- Red tikka powder (red powder used by Indian women to mark their heads), red clay, or red ochre (hematite clay dust)
- Music and rhythm makers, specifically a rattle and a drum
- Sacred objects you wish to bless in the full moonlight
- Crystals
- Bowls of sea water or sea salt added to water
- Paper and pen

This ceremony should be done at night under the light of the full moon. You may choose to perform this outside if it is warm enough; either inside or outside, create a space that is comfortable for sitting and lying down, whether for just yourself or others as well. Next, set up your space with soft, lush fabrics, heaps of sweet smelling and colorful flowers, the images and candles, incense, and bowls of water. Water reflecting moonlight enhances the power of the sacred ceremony. Sprinkle glitter to create a space with endless reflections. Anoint the space with essential oils such as sandalwood, lavender, rose, or jasmine.

Next, anoint yourself (and each other) with the fragrant oils. Use the tikka or clay to mark each other's chakra points. This red powder is a powerful and ancient symbol of the goddess and has been used by women for thousands of years; using it helps us to link ourselves to the millions of women who have been alive on this planet, practicing sacred worship under the full moon.

Then create the sacred space, first calling in the four directions. As you call in each direction and element, allow yourself to really feel the words drip from your tongue, to acknowledge the sacredness of speaking. Let the words themselves become offerings, your body become an offering to the goddess, the moon, the earth, to each other. Visualize each element moving into your body and expressing itself through you. For example, if you are calling fire and the south, really feel the warmth of the fire moving and blazing through your body, through the core of your being and radiating outward through your fingertips and toes. After calling each of the directions and presenting the offering, then call in mother earth, father sky, and the center. Take some time with these, allowing the power of them to seep into your body. Lastly, you will call in the moon, beckoning her to join the circle and enter your being, infuse you with her spirit.

Once you have called the directions, you can take a moment to write down any wishes that you want to manifest and put them on the altar. Think carefully of a few strong intentions that you wish to call into your life. Keep it simple, yet request the things you truly desire. The full moon energetically enhances all things and what you want to call in is magnified by its power.

Next, you will spend time raising the power of the sacred circle. This is done with the rattles, drum, and any other music makers as well as free toning or chanting. Start slowly with the sounds and let it build. Move your body, opening up the energy channels and freeing yourself to experience spirit.

When the priestess feels the power has been built up enough, she will motion to the main drummer or music maker to begin to slow it down. If you are alone, when you feel so intense that you may burst with love and power, begin to focus all of the energy raised into your heart space. Bring your breath and awareness into the heart and sit down; if you are in a group, form a circle. Visualize sending this incredible power and love that has been raised to help heal all beings and the planet. Spend several moments doing this.

Send the love as a powerful intention to manifest your wishes on the altar and bless your magical tools and items. Imagine each other whole, healed, and healthy; visualize the people you love—even the people you don't love—as well as your family and friends, your community, and the world receiving this powerful love and beauty that is radiating through your being.

Then, if you are alone, stand up to receive the full moonlight blessing. If you are in a group, the priestess will stand and call each person one by one to the center of the circle. There she will channel the power of the goddess from the moon and its beauty into you, using sound or mantra, gentle stroking or caressing, or pressing on points on your body. She will draw down this energy into your being and ask that the goddess bless you. If you are acting as the priestess, you will perform this role as if you are the goddess herself (which you are). Envision the moonlight shining down into each of the people you bring into the center of the group and anoint them with light and blessing. Use sounds such as "Ahhh…" or a simple mantra such as "Receive the blessing…" as you stroke and press the moonlight into each person's body. Imagine their entire aura filling up with brilliant, shimmering light and that they are healed and whole. While each person is in the center of the group, the circle should also visualize the moonlight pouring down into the person, filling them up with beautiful, loving, and healing light.

After each person has had a turn, the priestess then calls the moon down into herself. At this time, the priestess may choose to also envision light and moon energy entering her. She will again raise the power of love and the sacred feminine through her own body with the specific intention of using the energy to bless the entire group. You could imagine this as a kind of deep honoring of any intense natural earth phenomena such as a volcano, ocean waves, earthquake, or storm. The priestess envisions the energy moving upward into her heart and outward to bless the group, as well as the earth. This is both a blessing and a deep gratitude for receiving the sacred feminine.

When this is over, the priestess may rest for a while, then stand up and signal to close the circle. If you are alone, this is the time to release the elements and directions as well as thanking mother earth. Allow the sacred objects to remain on the altar to be blessed for three days in the moonlight.

six

THE BODHISATTVA
Developing Compassion

*Wherever in the Three Worlds a womanly form is
seen, that is said to be my form, whether she belongs
to a low family or not low... Each in her own form is
resolute in benefiting all living beings... When those
women are honored, they give [success] instantly to
those who desire the welfare of all beings. Therefore
one should honor women.*

—THE CANDAMAHAROSANA TANTRA

*Imagine you sit up upon the rock, filled to the brim with
vital life force from your beautiful garden, the flowing water
below, the warmth of the sun and the stone, the touch of a
loving spirit. The energy grows and grows within, becoming
a powerful sphere of love, a ball of immense loving potency.
You know intuitively that this loving energy is fueled by
your own power and love and capable of healing others as
well. Your guide or friend places his or her hands on your
back and you feel even more energy flow through you; it*

becomes so strong that you know you must share this inner love with others. You open your mouth and allow a long tone of beauty to come forth, emanating the love through your voice. You open your heart and hands and visualize this loving energy flowing through you and outward into your garden, then encompassing your canyon. Imagine this flowing, loving light moving out to the people you love, your community, your country, and finally the entire world. Offer this loving light as a gift to the mother earth in deep thanks for your path as a woman on this planet now. Offer yourself as a Bodhisattva to do the work needed to help all beings on earth find their own inner enlightenment. Know that you are loving and powerful.

As we move into the deepest aspects of love, supported by power and healing, we come to a place of inner wise loving. We are inspired by the loving wisdom held by the compassionate Bodhisattva. The Bodhisattva archetype is a loving being who forgoes his or her enlightenment for the sake of freeing all sentient beings from delusion and suffering. This kind of intense sacrifice is one of the most powerful forms of love on the planet and is akin to the deep love that a mother holds for her child. This is the loving aspect of the sacred feminine that acts from a place of pure open-heartedness, clarity, and with generosity that springs forward to positively affect others.

Our inner Bodhisattva is deeply empathic toward all beings on earth and can tap into the pain and suffering of those who have experienced loss, separation, sorrow, and trauma. This empathy is often expressed by women, both physically and psychologically. Our bodies and minds are hardwired to empathize with the world around us and nurture our family, friends, and community. This deep empathy is what Starhawk calls immanence and is similar to the concept of interconnectedness found in Buddhist philosophy.

When we flow with the awareness of our interconnectedness, our feeling of being separate in a space of suffering naturally dissolves into a loving presence. Our inner Bodhisattva reminds us we are connected to everything: the wind, the rain, the whales and their song, our lover, our children, the mountain, the breath that moves in and out of each of us.

The Bodhisattva not only sacrifices her own enlightenment, she is also committed to clearly understanding what will benefit others. Similarly, women often sacrifice aspects of their small selves to benefit the greater good, using their inner Bodhisattva. When we work with the truth of love, we find that often what people need is simpler than what we think they need. In other words, activating the inner Bodhisattva allows for a great spacious love to arise, one that can hear the woes and suffering of others and transmute that suffering into compassion by simply being present. In this chapter, Quan Yin takes the form of the Bodhisattva and offers help without personal recognition or expectation.

The Foundational Practice

After we have done ceremony and exercises to activate the Healer and Consort, we can form a more stable practice to focus our inner love with clarity and awareness. We do this by using breath and sitting meditation. Many of my students over the years say, "Oh, I tried to meditate but I just can't. My mind is running all over the place, I'll never be someone who meditates." But it is crucial to understand that *all* of us have minds that run all over the place, that jump from one thing to another. We dash to work, to home, to chores, to entertainment, then lie listless and check out, glad to be able to escape ourselves, without ever allowing ourselves to simply be. It is tiring just to think about! We may do heaps of ritual and circling and dancing and breathing, but if we have not really come to a place that is still and allowed our hearts to truly open, we will not know our truest, deepest joy. Disciplining ourselves to be still and quiet each day sows potent seeds for our hearts to open with compassion and experience the love of the inner Bodhisattva.

EXERCISE 6.1

Focusing on the Breath

A simple meditation that can help you center is based on what is available to all of us right now: the breath. This quiet practice enables you to be with yourself for a few moments and allows space into the chaotic mind. First thing in the morning is ideal, but any time is suitable. If you can sit each day at the same time, this helps to stabilize the practice and you will experience more benefits. Choose a space that is quiet where you won't be disturbed. Your altar space is perfect. If you are uncomfortable sitting on the floor, use a chair. The point is to be still and quiet without struggling too much. If you are fine on the floor, make sure you use cushions for support, so that it is easier to straighten your spine. If you can, sit in lotus, half lotus, or simply cross your legs. If you are in the chair, rest your feet flat on the floor. Keep your spine straight and relax your shoulders. Make sure your chin is slightly tucked in and rest your hands either on your knees or in your lap, your right hand inside your left. Notice any tension as you sit like this. You may feel tension immediately in your belly, back, or hips. Allow it to be there, do not judge or criticize. Bring your attention mindfully to the breath. Allow thoughts to float through the mind, like clouds in the sky. When you notice your mind wandering off and daydreaming, simply bring the attention back to the breath. You will do this hundreds of times in your first twenty minutes and it soon will become tiring. This is normal. This is a bit of work! Continue to bring your attention back to your breath. After sitting, trying not to move throughout, you may want to close the session with a simple dedication for the benefit of all beings or for the earth. This allows you to stretch your heart for a moment, to remember not to focus on yourself and to water the seed of compassion within.

Real meditation is not simply spacing out and having a nice dreamy bliss time, it is being with yourself right now and right here with what really is. It may take several weeks before you begin to notice a difference, but certainly you will. You may see that you are noticing your breath more often throughout the day, that you take time to be quiet between activities. With time you will come to cherish that quiet moment first thing in the morning, and eventually it will permeate your day and your being.

Quan Yin

All over Asia, people honor Quan Yin, the compassionate Bodhisattva who carries the pearls of loving illumination. Her name means She-Who-Hearkens-to-the-Cries-of-the-World. Like Mami Wata, she is associated with water and is shown pouring a stream of healing water from her vase, blessing beings with physical and spiritual peace. Like Mary and Artemis, she is considered a virgin and is a protectress for women. Quan Yin offers women a religious life as an alternative to marriage and grants children to those who want them. She is also a deity of the wild places, often appearing under a full moon, by ponds and willow trees, and brings rain and nourishment to those in need. Quan Yin evolved from the god Avalokiteshvara, worshipped in India and Tibet. When Avalokiteshvara was first worshipped in China thousands of years ago, he was in the Bodhisattva form of a male Buddha. By the twelfth century, he transformed from a male to a female goddess, the present Quan Yin, perhaps in response to the need for a deeper connection to the sacred feminine.

A Tale of Quan Yin
In the middle of the night, a woman awoke in intense labor and her baby was ready to be born. Her husband, frantic with fear and

excitement, prepared to go find the doctor for help. He rushed down to the village as clouds mounted in the distance threatening a terrible storm. At last he reached the doctor's house but was dismayed to discover that the doctor had gone to another village. He searched through the small town and finally found a midwife who was willing to come with him to help his struggling wife.

They hurriedly climbed the mountain together, but clouds continued to gather overhead and it began to snow. As they climbed, the snow swirled strongly, burying all the usual landmarks, and they wandered for some time, losing their way. The husband grew more anxious when he realized they were wandering around in circles. Suddenly, distinctly, they heard the tinkling sound of small bells. He stopped and motioned the midwife to stop. "Do you hear that?" he asked. She nodded, and they paused, exhausted from their efforts.

Out of the white darkness appeared a beautiful woman. Her face was round and illuminated like the moon. "Are you lost?" she asked. They nodded, too awed to answer, and she smiled, saying, "Follow me."

The man and the midwife followed the lovely woman who glowed in the night. Her shine illuminated the path and melted the snow a bit, making it easier for them to follow the trail behind her. They seemed to arrive at the man's home in no time and the midwife rushed in to the wife, who was wailing in her birth pain. The man paused and looked at the beautiful woman, saying, "Won't you come in? It's so cold out!"

"No, I have to go on." The snow was lessening, and her beautiful, illuminated form stood out more clearly against the dark night cloaked in snow.

"Let me at least get you a warm drink," he said and dashed inside to prepare hot tea. He peeked in at his wife who was calm now, her face relaxed, holding the midwife's hand and resting between contractions. The husband went into the kitchen, heated up the water, and prepared the tea.

When he returned to the door, the snow had stopped. With the tea in hand, he looked out and realized that the glowing woman was gone. The quiet night held only the moon now, and he could clearly see the footprints that led up to the door. With a start he realized there were only two sets of footprints, his own and the midwife's. A sudden wonder overwhelmed him and he pressed his hand to his heart. He knew it was Quan Yin who had assisted them that night, then disappeared as quietly and quickly as she had appeared.

Keys to the Tale

This is a simple and beautiful story that illustrates the loving qualities of compassionate guidance embodied by Quan Yin. The husband represents the part of us that may feel completely overwhelmed at times in our lives when we need help. Sometimes, help does not come in the form we expect, as the man finds a midwife instead of a doctor. In stressful situations, we may need to stay open to the kind of help we may receive.

Quan Yin, the goddess of childbirth, shows up in association with a midwife. When the husband cannot find the male doctor, he turns to the female midwife to help his wife. As sisters, daughters, and later midwives, women assisted birth for tens of thousands of years. We know that in past cultures, and in some remaining traditional cultures today, women are still primarily assisted by women as they birth children. As the patriarchy rose into power, and male doctors became the norm even for women's health, midwives were still the birth assistants and herbal healers for the common people. Later, they were completely displaced by doctors and often demonized by the establishment. Many were certainly burned on the witches' stake during the Inquisition. Still, in times of need, villagers would turn to the midwives, knowing they could rely on their wisdom, which was continuously being threatened. Quan Yin, although often portrayed as quiet and peaceful, is powerfully reminding us to reconnect with the feminine wisdom that has helped birth humans for a long time. In this way, this tale reminds us to be open to assistance that comes from a source that is imbued with the sacred feminine.

After the man finds the midwife, they begin to climb up the mountain, but the snow becomes treacherous and landmarks are indistinguishable. Even on the most familiar paths, we can become lost. Snow, like the goddess, is both beautiful and threatening in this situation. She can confound us with her beauty and make the world unrecognizable. The goddess can also appear at a moment's notice and guide our way, which Quan Yin does, with the tinkling of bells and moonlit radiance, asking the man and midwife if they are lost. As the Bodhisattva of compassion, she hears and answers the cries of all beings. This book encourages you to call in your guides in the form of ancestors and spirit guardians to help in times of crisis. Often we fall back into the habitual patterns of looking for help in the standard, Western way of the physical reality, but it is useful to remember that help can appear in many forms, such as guides, dreams, and omens.

When they arrive back home, the midwife is able to soothe the wife quickly, reduce her pains, and begin accompanying her on the birth journey. The husband offers tea to Quan Yin, but when he brings it to her, she has gone, disappeared into the snowy night leaving behind no trace, not even her footsteps. This is the beauty of a true Bodhisattva, one who simply shows up and guides the way. She needs no thanks, no gratitude, no acknowledgement of her helpfulness. She is on her way again to assist others, having done what was necessary. This is a vast kind of love, one that does not rely on ego and is given unconditionally. According to Sogyal Rinpoche, a Tibetan Buddhist teacher, "What the world needs more than anything is active servants of peace...dedicated to their bodhisattva vision and to the spreading of wisdom into all reaches of our experience."[21] We all have access to this clear guiding light inside and can call on it to help others in times of crisis. Sometimes it is good practice to help others specifically without them knowing it was you. Then we are not motivated by the need for recognition, but instead practice giving unconditionally.

The Bodhisattva asks us to nourish ourselves and fill our hearts so full that the compassion and love naturally overflow outwardly to the world. When we work to help others, we are practicing karma yoga, or selfless service. Every ashram I have stayed in requires you to perform karma yoga as a way to help out. The goal of this action is to recognize that the simple act of giving service is all the gratitude we need. By learning to cultivate compassion through helping others, we reduce our small self, or ego, and thus become even more filled with love. This can take many forms, and each of us has a particular way to do this through our specific gifts and talents. Quan Yin reminds us to effortlessly serve others in a way that is both joyous and illumined, but without expectation, without needing thanks or appreciation. This is the true work of a Bodhisattva, someone whose every action is performed with clear intention, from the heart.

When our love becomes so powerful, it is like a fire, reaching out to ignite many people of the world. Obstacles are more easily removed, and we can face challenges with strength and grace. The Bodhisattva inspires us to take up the blazing fires of love, to open our hearts so wide that they may burst, and love the world so intensely that it changes and heals and transforms.

---

21. Sogyal Rinpoche, *The Tibetan Book of Living and Dying*, p. 368.

Deep Listening

This is another exercise that connects you to inner stillness and the Bodhisattva within. All it requires is a commitment to one day of deep listening. This means that you spend the entire day mindfully being aware of how you pay attention to others. It means that you quietly hold space for them and what they are saying and communicating to you. When you do speak, you can communicate from a place of intention and nourishment.

Choose one day to practice deep listening. When people tell you their stories, issues, and concerns, try not to relate their story to one of your own. Although this is a normal way of connecting to people, try to simply hear their story and hold space for their process. This is not a passive quality, but a kind of active listening. Think of Quan Yin as you do this practice, the Bodhisattva who hears the cries of help, turns up when needed, listens actively, then disappears again. Notice your own mind and how quick it is to jump in with information to add to a conversation, tell your own story, or respond with emotion. Instead of voicing these thoughts, allow them to simply pass through you while in connection with others. This may take some practice. Each time you do add your own comment, notice when you do, and see if it comes from a place of compassion or ego.

In many cultures, including Native American and Tibetan, not saying much is usually associated with wisdom. This is because the deep listener can also see the essence of things and simply be present with what is without commenting on it. This is not easy for many of us, growing up in a world that has continuous running commentary from a variety of mediums. This practice can be even more beneficial if you also refrain from active commenting on your social networking sites and taking instant digital photos, and minimize your phone conversations. We often spend a lot of hours commenting on the world and not as much time simply *being* in the world. All wisdom and insight come from being; very little comes from chatting.

This exercise can be done throughout the day and not just with other people but with all sounds around you, including both city and natural sounds. As you listen to these sounds, attempt to not judge them but just notice the variety of tones, conversations, music, and other sounds that float through your world. Practice this deep listening once a month to help relieve your mind from its chattering state and allow the art of surrender to move you into a place of quiet and insight. As you practice this, you will find a measure of peace and a deep reservoir of love that wells up within you and naturally pours out to others in your life.

Women Around the World

I spent more than seven years living and traveling throughout India. My husband and I spent much of that time living in Kerala, South India. After the death of our first daughter, Rubybleu Puja, we founded a small nonprofit called the Rubybleu Foundation to help women and children of India and Nepal. We mostly raised funds to give scholarships to girls in higher education, assisted women's groups in ways to earn extra income for their families, and also gave yearly donations to a health clinic outside of Kathmandu, Nepal. These projects were tiny, really, in the face of larger world problems, but they taught me a lot about women in the third world and women who are indigenous to the land and local culture. Many of these women suffer from intense poverty, suppression, and lack of health and education.

Statistically, women who are educated and empowered have fewer children, which is one of the first crucial steps to changing some of these problems. Women tend to think outside themselves, to care for their family, their children, the community at large. Time and time again when we visited various self-help women's groups in South India the main complaint was that when the men did make money, it was often spent on alcohol instead of food, medicine, and household supplies. Conversely, when women are given money in the form of microloans they have a high payback rate, as high as 95 percent in some areas of the world. India is currently rooted in a deep patriarchy, one that requires sons to take over the family, care for the aging parents, and give the daughters up in marriage. This system disempowers women so extensively that millions of baby girls are murdered each year, routine abortions of females are common, and girls have less access to education, health care, and social freedom. Ironically, some of the most empowered feminist women I met were Catholic nuns, many of whom had left the crushing oppression of Hinduism in favor of the life of a nun—where they could do social work that they loved and avoid marriage altogether!

Women have come a long way in the last century, but there is a lot more to do. An integral development of the inner Bodhisattva is to not only heal ourselves, but to reach out and lift others as well. Working with the women of India through my foundation provided some of the most powerful experiences of my life. Although women are suffering there, many also have an incredible community even in the face of great adversity. This is very inspiring for someone who comes from a land that is full of (apparent) freedom and immense wealth. I recommend that you become more educated on the women's issues around the world as they are really all of our issues. Some great organizations that are working with women include the Global Fund for Women and CARE, listed in the resources section of this book. Remembering that we are all connected and taking action to help empower women is loving action that activates the Bodhisattva within.

A Ceremony to Send Healing

This is a simple ceremony to send healing love to others. Be sure to ask permission before performing a ceremony such as this. If you cannot get permission, do not send healing to a person; instead, choose to send healing to the earth.

Gather together the following items:

- Four candles for the four cardinal directions
- Offerings for the directions as well as offerings for mother earth, father sky, and center
- A separate, larger candle to symbolize healing energy
- A picture or symbol of what you plan to send healing to, either the person or a picture of the earth

Decorate your altar with healing, soothing colors and perhaps include an image of Quan Yin, Mami Wata, or other healing deity.

Turn off the lights and light a candle to focus your gaze. Call in the four directions as well as earth, sky, and center to create sacred space. Then take a moment to ground yourself. If you know a specific grounding exercise, you can use that. Otherwise, you can become grounded through your breath and being aware of your body. Close your eyes and tune into the breath. Allow your awareness to drop down into the base of the spine, where your sit bones are touching the chair or cushion. Focus the breath on this area for a few moments, intending a sense of grounding or connectedness to the earth. You can imagine a cord of light extending from your body into the earth, connecting you to the pulse or rhythm of the planet. Focus your breath down through this cord into the very center of the earth, imagining energy coming up from the earth and into your body. Feel the warmth and presence of the earth in your body for a few moments. This will keep you grounded and connected to the earth as you perform your healing work.

Once you feel grounded, face the image and candle and state aloud that your healing intention is for the benefit of the recipient or the earth. Then hold up your hands, facing the image and close your eyes. You may keep your hands raised in the air or rest them on your knees, but keep the palms facing the image. If you are healing the earth, you may hold your palms facing downward toward the earth's surface. It is important to remain comfortable, so see what works best. Concentrate on the breath for a few moments.

As you breathe in, imagine yourself filling with golden, clear light from the earth below you and the sky above you. Allow this clear light to fill up in your heart center for several minutes. Let the golden light grow larger and larger, filling up the entire room. Then, when you feel completely full of this light, imagine it moving through space toward the recipient. You can either imagine the recipient there in front of you, or simply look at the picture and imagine it flowing into the image. Continue sending the light with the breath for ten to fifteen minutes. As you inhale, imagine yourself continuously filling up with light; as you exhale, it flows into the person or the earth. Visualize the person or the earth healthy and relieved of illness or issue. See him or her dancing in joy and light or see the earth healthy and full of vital life force. Then, close the healing connection by stating aloud, "This healing session is now finished. I disengage from healing." This is to make sure we do not stay connected and brings us back to the present moment. If you feel the need to, you may dedicate the practice to all beings, so that it helps everyone in the universe. When you are finished, blow out the healing candle. Finally, release the directions and dissolve the sacred space.

SEVEN

THE WEAVER
Spinning the World into Being

What occurs around you and within you reflects your
own mind and shows you the dream you are weaving.
—VEN. DHYANI YWAHOO, ETOWAH CHEROKEE

Imagine sitting in your garden, suffused with love and
power. Light and energy radiate out of you effortlessly and
embrace the entire world with their glowing beauty and
strength. There is a feeling of immense love as you expe-
rience the connectedness of all things. Your own body and
mind and heart are intricately woven into your garden,
your canyon, the people in your life, the entire earth. All
that you are is simply a microcosm of the entire universe and
thus, you are filled with a loving power that unlocks the sacred
feminine wisdom within. As you continue to sit on your rock,
focusing on your breath in and out, you see strands of light
emerging from your heart and connecting with people, places,
and events in your life. These strands are your specific con-
nections to your own path in this lifetime. You send each of

the connections a measure of love, acting as the wise Weaver
and holding space for creating the most powerful and loving
life possible.

Our inner garden is infused with love as well as power as we come into the realm of wisdom. As we connect with our gifts, we learn to use them through wise action by calling on the Weaver archetype. The Weaver is more than a woman who weaves cloth; she is one who weaves energy, ideas, and wisdom into manifestation. The Weaver has deep roots in the sacred feminine and inspires us to activate our inner connections as well as our community. We are multidimensional beings, and the inner Weaver helps us bring those parts together to honor them as a whole woman. When we weave our gifts, powers, and love into our daily lives, we become more in touch with the wisdom of the sacred feminine.

The inner Weaver understands that her life is one small strand in the great web of human and earthly existence; that she is simultaneously a multidimensional being and a tiny speck in the infinite vastness of the universe. The Weaver also has the capability to see the small details as well as the larger picture. Thus the Weaver challenges us to recognize the wisdom that we are not only connected, but together responsible for our communities and our world. When we activate our wise inner Weaver, we better understand our place in the universe manifest as a thread in the web, rather than an isolated, separate person.

All over the world, women weave traditional cloth that shows the group they belong to, which people they came from, what part of the earth they resonate with. Stories abound with spinners and weavers, and this archetype is often linked to the spinners of fate, the creators of the universe, and the markers of time. Countless myths speak of a weaver of time, a dancer, a creator, a being that spins the world into being. The Weaver comes to us in the form of Spider Woman in the myth below, carrying the wisdom of creating in balance and harmony.

Women naturally weave in a variety of ways of "multitasking," bringing together different activities, conversations, and insights when in a group. If we sit back and watch the way women network, exchange recipes and ideas, helping with the children, we can see how language developed from these very intimate relationships. This is also seen when we observe the biological differences in men's and women's brains. Dean Falk, a specialist in brain evolution, "took note of the smaller (by 10 percent on average) size of the human female brain today, as opposed to the male, but pointed out that the female brain is larger *in proportion to body size* than is the male brain and has just as many neurons. In addition, the female brain is differently 'wired' than the male brain. For example, three pathways that connect the two hemispheres of the brain, especially the larger pathway called the corpus callosum, are proportionately larger in the female brain."[22] Women link many more ideas, thoughts, emotions, and memories together simultaneously; they tend to knit ideas together when circling, adding to the mix rather than competing for attention.

<u>EXERCISE 7.1</u>

Weaving Womb, Heart, and Head

This exercise enables you to connect your heart with your womb. This helps to release tension and connect the deeper, sacred feminine within your body to your heart center. This can also be done with a group of women, using visualization to weave wombs and hearts together around the circle. Even if women have had their wombs and/or ovaries removed, they can still sit envisioning the space where their womb once was, honoring that part of her, feeling

---

22.   J. M. Adovasio, Olga Soffer, and Jake Page, *The Invisible Sex*, p. 111.

the space still held by the vagina and cervix. The description that follows is for a group; you can adapt it as necessary for solo work.

Sit in a circle, relaxed with eyes closed. One woman should verbally lead the group through the exercise. Focus on the breath for several moments, allowing tension to spiral away, down into the earth. After some time, begin to visualize your womb, or the area of the second chakra. Imagine it filling up with golden, brilliant, warm, healing light. As you breathe in, the light becomes brighter and more energizing. As you breathe out, it radiates outward from your center into the circle. Focus on this image with breathing for several minutes. Then imagine filaments of light extending out from your womb into the other women's wombs in the room. Imagine you are braiding these strings of light together, weaving one another with light and love. Continue focusing on your breathing as well, imagining the light brilliant with each inhale and extending out and around the circle with each exhale. When you are doing this, you may want to also add sound to the exercise, allowing the sound to come from your womb, the tone that it resonates with. Let this sound come naturally, without thinking about it, just up and out from the center of your being as a woman. Continue womb-weaving for several minutes, imagining the room filled with woven threads of light, hearing and delighting in the sound of women giving a voice to their wombs.

Then shift your awareness into your heart. Just as you did with the womb, imagine a brilliant light emanating from your heart center. As you do this, the sound will naturally change into the openness of the heart space. Again, imagine threads of light emerging from your heart and weaving around the circle and merging with the other women's hearts. Allow the sound and light and breath to continue here for several minutes.

Then bring the awareness up into your head, repeating the exercise with threads of light emerging from your third eye. Shift the sound into one tone that is more concentrated. Envision the light weaving around the circle and joining with the other women's third eyes, connecting one another in a powerful space of wombs, hearts, and minds. Spend several minutes toning and visualizing the brilliant, warm light. Then extend the threads outward, encompassing the entire circle with brilliant strings of light. Finally, together, all chant one sound, such as the Aum or the Ah sound. This helps to connect the energy simultaneously and ground it. When you are finished, you may choose to put your hands and/or head on the floor or ground where you are sitting to help bring yourself back into ordinary awareness.

The Sacred Weaver

The goddess as the Weaver—weaver of cloth, fates, destiny, the universe, the very fabric of life—is found in countless myths, fairy tales, and stories. In pre-dynastic Egypt, Neith was the goddess of weaving, and her emblem was the loom shuttle that is often figured above her head. The Japanese sun goddess Amaterasu works at her weaving loom in the sky, as does Saule, the life-affirming sun goddess of the Baltic peoples. She is believed to spin the sunbeams into being. The Celtic goddess Brigid is, among other things, a weaver. Frigg, the goddess of the Norse, spins in Scandinavian skies, and her distaff is the constellation of Orion's Belt. These goddesses all figure strongly in ancient myth, weaving the world into being.

The Weaver is able to weave the stories of not only humans, but all living things in her loom. Sjöö and Mor point out the importance of weaving and storytelling through the use of ancient textiles, stating that "a highly charged symbol language was used to communicate herstory and myth. Spinning and weaving were imbued with magic powers, and inscribed spindle-whorls are found in innumerable Neolithic sacrificial pits sacred to the Goddess."[23] Today, in Mayan cultures in Guatemala, women still weave the creation story into their woolen ponchos. Using brilliant colored threads, they depict images of the first life on earth, water, trees, animals, and people to show where they came from, who they belong to, what part of the earth they connect with. Then they wear it! How beautiful to not only wear what we have created, but to wear the story from which we came. In other parts of the world, the tradition of weaving is still essential to a myriad of cultures.

To spin a yarn is indeed to spin a tale, a story of good and evil, of lovers, of how things came to be. Thus, stories, art, weaving, and spinning are intricately entwined and inseparable from each other. Many of us have lost our connection to the woven cloth, the weaving or dance of life, and I encourage you to explore that further within your women's circle and in your community. Each time people get together they weave, and honoring diversity means honoring all the strands, all the aspects of the web.

The story below tells how Wandering Girl became Weaving Woman. This story, as well as many others from Native American myth, figures Spider Woman, the great weaver of the world. She gives Wandering Girl not only the knowledge of how to weave, but the wisdom of how to keep harmony and balance in life.

The Story of Weaving Woman[24]
The old ones tell a story of Wandering Girl who became Weaving Woman and what happened when she did not follow Spider Woman's warning. From the beginning of time, Spider Woman knew the secret of spinning and weaving.

---

23. Sjöö and Mor, p. 51.

24. This story by Lois Duncan is adapted here with her permission from the following source: Lois Duncan and Shonto Bigay (illustrator), *The Magic of Spider Woman*. New York: Scholastic, 1996.

Among the people, there was one girl called Wandering Girl because she was a shepherd and wandered all over the hills letting her flocks graze. She was strong-willed and stubborn as well. Boy with a Dream loved her very much and secretly hoped to make her his wife one day.

Then the great Spirit Being came to the world one summer and taught the people how to hunt, grow crops, and build shelters. Spirit Being also taught them the ceremonial chants and songs so they could bless all of their work and live in harmony with the earth.

Meanwhile, Wandering Girl spent the summer grazing her flocks in the hills, oblivious to the teachings given by Spirit Being. When the leaves began to fall from the branches and the cold winds began to blow, Wandering Girl returned to her people, but found they were all snug in their homes keeping warm by the fire. Wandering Girl called to Spirit Being for help, shivering and alone in the cold. Spirit Being did not respond, but Spider Woman heard her cries.

Spider Woman said, "I can teach you to make blankets from the wool of your sheep. Then you will stay warm." Spider Woman showed her how to shear the sheep and spin the wool into thread. Then Spider Woman told her, "Now you will no longer be called Wandering Girl, but Weaving Woman, and you will weave warm blankets for your people. This will benefit your people greatly. But you must promise one thing," cautioned Spider Woman. "Living on earth you must always remember that you are learning to walk the Middle Way. This means honoring the path of balance and not doing too much of one thing. So, remember to never weave too much or too long."

Weaving Woman agreed to Spider Woman's words. It grew even colder, and she wondered how she would weave in such frigid snowy weather. Boy with a Dream saw her standing in the cold and offered his home to her, and they became husband and wife. So Boy with a Dream became Man Who Is Happy.

All winter, Weaving Woman wove the blankets that were the colors of winter: black and gray drab tones. She often put aside her work, honoring Spider Woman's caution. But when spring came, the world exploded into green leaves and glorious colored flowers. Inspired, Weaving Woman began to make dyes to enrich her blankets with beautiful colors. She wove in the beautiful colors of the sky, the sunset, and the rainbow. Her blankets began to tell stories of the birds and animals filled with radiance and song.

Overjoyed by color, she decided to weave a special blanket for Spirit Being using every color of the world. She set to work on this special blanket, so impassioned by her ideas that she wove and wove, without stopping. She awoke at sunrise and wove until sundown day after day.

Her husband grew worried and reminded her of Spider Woman's warning. As he watched his wife, Man Who Is Happy became Man Who Is Frightened. Yet Weaving Woman did not listen and continued to weave her gorgeous blanket, saying she was almost finished. But that evening, when her husband returned from the hunt, he found his beautiful wife on the floor, unable to move.

He covered her with blankets and called for Hand Trembler, the shaman, to help. Hand Trembler made offerings and said prayers to ask Spirit Being for help. Then a voice rose out of the blanket that was still on the loom. "I am here," called Weaving Woman, "my spirit is here, trapped in the blanket."

Hand Trembler said, "She has broken her promise to Spider Woman and woven herself into her own blanket." He made more offerings to determine how to help Weaving Woman.

Man Who Is Frightened saw his wife stuck in the blanket, the spirit of her face in terror, trapped by her own creative work. "We must help her!" he cried to the shaman. "How can we set her free?"

"We can help her only if Spider Woman makes the blanket less than perfect. Spider Woman must have permission to make a flaw in the blanket," said the shaman.

Weaving Woman called from the blanket, "Yes, Spider Woman, you have my permission to make the blanket less than perfect." Spider Woman reached out and pulled a long thread from the blanket, creating a spirit pathway for Weaving Woman. Weaving Woman came rushing out of the blanket and returned to her body. She leapt up and embraced her husband.

"I have learned my lesson!" she cried. "Never again will I weave too long." After that she called all the weaver women together and told them her story. "We must honor Spider Woman's wise words and never become too proud or obsessed by our own making. Let us always make one flaw in our blankets to serve as a reminder to keep humble with our work," she told the women. Since then, every blanket of the Navajo people has a flaw in it so that the weaver's beauty and spirit will not remain with the blanket.

Keys to the Tale[25]

The story begins with Wandering Girl tending to her flocks. In Native American traditions, people are named for the way they relate to each other, with the tribe, and/or with the land. The name is not a fixed thing and changes as the way the person relates to the world changes. This kind of name describes oneself as a strand in the web of life and names the expression we are offering to the world. In Western culture, we can be inspired by this view that is needed to weave our world into a place of harmony. When we see ourselves as separate from the earth, we destroy and consume too much without staying in balance. We can relate this interconnectedness to our own daily lives by witnessing people, our house,

---

25. These are some keys to the myths upon which Lois Duncan based her story about Weaving Woman.

and our land as part of ourselves. Perhaps we can think of a name that describes the way we relate to people or the world around us. This name is changeable as well—just as Wandering Girl's name changes, so can our own way of relating to the world. This gives us immense freedom. We do not have to stay fixed to one way of being; we can actively choose to transform or change our way of relating to the world just as we can choose how we want to weave the tapestry of our lives.

In the story, the people receive special gifts from Great Spirit, learning how to build their homes, plant and harvest foods, and, most importantly, how to stay balanced and in harmony with the earth. Wandering Girl misses out on these lessons, though, and is literally left out in the cold, unsure what to do next. Many of us have times in our lives when we feel like Wandering Girl, feeling that we have missed out on something, that we are not sure what our role is in our society or in the world web as a whole. This is especially common in a culture that places less emphasis on community and more on maintaining a middle-class lifestyle. When we feel lost or displaced, our vital life force suffers and we can be overwhelmed with coldness in the form of depression, illness, fatigue, or apathy. In these times, we must open to the gifts of those around us, to receive guidance from people, nature, and spirit.

Spider Woman comes to Wandering Girl and teaches her a special skill: how to spin wool and weave using the wool from her own flock. She is given a gift of how to make use of her own resources. This is a key to finding what nourishes our spirit and how we can contribute to our community. Things we have in our possession, are drawn to, or love are usually clear indications of our own natural gifts and ways to work in the world web. This is our personal, unique wisdom that we have to offer to the whole.

Spider Woman is a reflection of the Weaver as the harbinger of culture. In many myths around the world, it is a woman or a goddess who gives the gifts of culture and civilization to human beings. Inanna brought the culture Mes from the underworld; Spider Woman brought the light to the earth by capturing the sun in a woven bag. We must ask ourselves, what is our special gift? Who might we open to for learning new ways of being or relating to the world? In Exercise 7.2 below, you can begin to discover and cultivate your special skills and talents and what you have to offer to the world. Sometimes, simply being receptive allows for gifts to emerge; other times we can actively seek out groups, classes, or ideas that inspire us and work to incorporate more of that in our own lives.

Wandering Girl needs a home and one is offered by Boy with a Dream, who becomes Man Who Is Happy. This event symbolizes the shift from girlhood to womanhood. Wandering Girl has found her inner gifts and is then offered the support of a home and a man to allow those gifts to come forth. Man Who Is Happy represents the part of us that has been transformed and anchored into power and love, as discussed in the previous chapters. When our inner selves can open up to honor our gifts, happiness and wisdom naturally arise.

Weaving Woman begins her life's work as a weaver. This is both an archetype, such as the ones explored in other parts of the book, as well as a very real and practical role in traditional communities. Sjöö and Mor note that weavers in the Navajo tradition "experience themselves as being directly inspired by the Great Spider Woman, the original weaver of the universe. They use no set patterns and feel no separation between art (sacred) and craft (secular, profane). The woven blankets are valued as organic expressions of the special powers of the makers. Each blanket with its inspired design has a spiritual significance, and is thought of as giving power and protection to the person who wears it."[26] This is similar to the way women in Africa make pots. Malidoma Patrice Somé discusses pottery-making events where women sing and chant and converse all day

---

26. Sjöö and Mor, p. 51.

long over their blocks of clay. Then in a sudden flurry of activity several pots are born out of the clay toward the end of the day. By connecting in with the spirit of the pots, the wisdom of the clay and earth can be heard and utilized in creation. This process is an extension of their own song, connectedness, and storytelling, just as traditional weaving is a way of telling the stories of one's people and their relation to the land.

Similarly, in Laos, the women weave their own skirts, each village with its unique pattern and way of expressing itself. The women wear these gorgeous hand-woven skirts as normal day wear, to harvest rice, clean the home, and tend the babies. To spend such care and time on one's own garments holds the wisdom of honoring the earth. How different this is from today's world of mass production and uniform products! Instead of using things that have been literally made and woven with love, we are wearing mechanization. This extends to include not only our clothing or pots but our music, our art, and even our food, the very things that should deeply nourish us. Weaver Woman inspires us to reexamine our relations to our world and all of the creations that are produced.

Weaver Woman is thrilled by the arrival of spring and delights in using its colors to dye her blankets, creating new patterns and stories. Spider Woman warned her to stay in balance and walk the middle way, yet in her excitement to weave the most beautiful blanket, she is overtaken by the blanket itself, losing her soul to it. This is a reminder to stay grounded and balanced even when we are doing something we passionately adore. This helps us to stay in harmony with our world. Overconsumption and overworking can drain us of our energy and leave us for dead, just as they do to Weaver Woman.

Also, this is a good reminder of the cycles of life. There are natural ebbs and flows in all aspects of life: with money, in creative process, with family and friends, while working, and so on. When in right balance, our bodies follow a natural process of activity, then rest, activity, then rest. Our society values production over anything else, and inaction is seen as devoid of value. But to honor both ourselves and our earth, we must have times of rest, just as the fields need to lay fallow. These times are when we gather for the next cycle of production and activity. If we do not take time for rest, nourishment, and renewal, we will become overworked.

In the final words of the story, we find that even today Navajo weavers always leave a flaw in their blankets, to let the soul escape. Besides reminding us to stay in right balance, this also advises us with the wisdom that we do not have to be perfect all the time. If we find ourselves tirelessly striving to create the perfect life, product, company, or project, we will often disappoint ourselves. Our pride can get the best of us in these situations, which will inevitably lead to feelings of inadequacy. Remembering that not everything must be exact; the house does not have to be perfectly clean; our art can contain flaws or even mistakes keeps us anchored in wisdom. This is part of spirit just as much as perfection. When I sing, I have a tendency to waver on the tune or fall out of rhythm. I am reminded of the ocean waves, which do not follow a precise mechanic rhythm. This is an essential wisdom of the Weaver, that we are part of the great whole, flaws and all.

EXERCISE 7.2

Preparing Your Vision

This exercise is done in preparation for the ceremony below where you will create a sacred braid. The purpose of the sacred braid is to manifest a vision through holding clear intention and weaving it in a form. This is an act of power, created with love in response to your inner wisdom. This is a symbolic ritual to dream your world into being. You are cultivating your inner Weaver and enabling your truth to energetically be spun out and into the world. This vision is not a mantra or a basic intention, it is a bigger dream of a life and incorporates several intentions all at once. For example, you may want to envision yourself joyfully expressing art, filled with health, owning a new car, and letting go of a negative habit all at once. The Weaver challenges us to hold our multidimensional dream as wise counsel enabling us to live a bigger dream.

Spend an entire month really thinking about your intentions, special dreams, and heart wisdom. I encourage you to take time to explore deeper into your inner wisdom and come up with a powerful and loving intention. To do this, use your time over the course of the month writing lists, making a collage, and/or envisioning what you would like to call into your life. Use the powers that you have learned so far walking the path of the sacred feminine. Think symbolically about your talents, essences, gifts, and personal wisdom. Perhaps you want to use symbols from your guardian spirits, ancestors, goddesses you have discovered, or myths you are working with. As you do this, collect nine small items you wish to represent the deeper aspects of this intention, sacred things that have been given to you or things you have found over the years. These should be small enough to tie into a braid (about a foot long) in the weaving ceremony. Perhaps collect nine for the archetypes in this book or, more simply, three for power, three for love, and three for wisdom. Once you have a clear sense of your vision, you are ready to perform the ceremony.

Weaving Ceremony: Sacred Braid

This simple, but powerful ceremony is done to dream your self more firmly into being. By creating a sacred art piece such as a braid, you are symbolically allowing your soul to speak to you its longings and inner dreams. The intention for this exercise is to name your unique sacred feminine qualities and celebrate them in a sacred braid. You can also do this with any kind of weaving activity such as making a dream catcher, hair wrap, blanket, or scarf, but be sure you have enough time to begin and complete the entire object during your ceremony.

Make sure there is enough light to work by. Prepare your altar with images that speak to you of your vision—your collage and lists as well as symbols or goddesses that represent weaving and interconnectedness. Gather the following items

- Offerings and candles for all seven directions
- Three colors of yarn (perhaps black, red, and white, the colors of the triple goddess) or more; use colors you feel coonected to
- Nine sacred items that you can attach to your braid of yarn, each one representing an intention or aspect of your intentions and sacred dream work

Create sacred space as you have done in the previous ceremonies, calling in the directions and giving offerings.

Begin to weave your sacred braid or create your woven vision. As you weave your braid, add in your special objects. Envision your intentions and clear heart dream while you do this process. You may want to sing a song or chant a mantra as you weave, using the sacred power of words and music to enhance your braid. Take your time, really invest your energy into your work. Do not worry about making the object perfect; this is an act of power and should be held with love as you make it, knowing it will serve as a wise reminder of your sacred feminine being. As you create your braid, be open to feelings and images that arise in your mind, which will also be infused in your spirit gift.

When you are finished weaving the braid with the objects, hold it to your heart and imagine it filling with light. This weaving is a representation of your power, your love, and your wisdom on your path of the sacred feminine. It is symbolic of your ability to begin to dream your life into being, a life that is based in courage, compassion, and clarity, all qualities of the goddess, yourself in the shape of a woman. You can use this sacred braid as the starter of a *mesa*, or sacred pouch, to be used in healing sessions, during initiatory work, or to manifest more strongly your own power and desires. Traditionally, a mesa is a bundle of potent objects used by healers and shamans to enhance their work. This is also a good place to store any oracle you might use such as tarot cards, as well as crystals, power objects given to you, and pictures of teachers or deities that inspire you. When you travel, it is helpful to bring your mesa with you for enhanced connections to others, healing, and clarity of your purpose. Whenever you do ceremony, keep your sacred braid on your altar and it will be charged by the energy and power raised up during the ceremony. During healing sessions for yourself, you may wish to lay the braid across an area that needs more healing. You may also use it to enhance dreams by placing it under your pillow at night. I have often found that my dreams slow down and become more clear when I use power objects I have made that live in my mesa. This braid also works as protection and can be placed on your altar to provide protection and guidance as you move more deeply into the sacred feminine path.

EiGHt

THE PRIESTESS
Navigating Between the Worlds

Ageless I stepped out of the sky
Touched down into the sea
Saw my image/In the reflection of the Sun…
We are One!
—Necia Desiree Harkless[27]

Imagine sitting quietly, imbued with power and wisdom, holding the space of loving connectedness to all your relations and to the earth. You feel the infinite wisdom of the vast cosmic web streaming through you and its profound loving energy that moves through all living things. Now imagine that your guides come to visit. They may come as specific beings, goddesses or gods, forms of light, or simply as a loving presence. Imagine they surround you as you continue to sit on the rock in quiet wisdom. Their light and love infuse you with an even deeper wisdom. Then you begin to travel

---

27.   Necia Desiree Harkless, "Evolution," from *Poems and Heart Images*.

up and out of the garden, taking flight to move through the dreamtime. Perhaps you take the shape of a flying bird or grow wings as you move up into the skies and travel over the landscape. Ask for a vision of the dreamtime, one that shows you who you are and why you are here. Be open to the messages that come from your guides, whether in the form of images, sound, or simply knowing. Ask your guides to take you to another power spot, one that holds information from the cosmos. Perhaps it is a sacred stone or living altar; it may be high on a cliff or mountain. Imagine receiving powerful, loving, and wise information from this sacred spot in the dreamtime as a priestess. Visualize yourself in the role of leader, space holder, and enabler. Remember what you are told and know that you can revisit this sacred wisdom place, just as you can revisit your sacred garden for healing and love.

As we move more deeply into a place of wisdom, we encounter our inner Priestess. The Priestess is the culmination of our practice with the sacred feminine. She is the visionary, the loving healer, the empowered warrior, the sacred weaver all rolled into one. She is the part of us that can see the broader picture, dip her ladle of understanding into antiquity, and pour it forth across the world which is thirsty for the reclaiming of the sacred feminine. Our inner Priestess has traveled a long journey and uncovered many sacred and nourishing spots along the way and knows it is time to share her wisdom.

The Priestess is akin to a shaman, one who is able to see in the dark. The Priestess archetype is often figured in the Tarot deck standing between two pillars: one of light and one of dark. She effectively navigates between these two worlds, the seen and unseen, the negative and positive, the masculine and feminine, the sacred and the profane, the sexual and the spiritual. Not only is she able to straddle these worlds, she is also at the very center of sacred space, carrying with her a deep understanding of the four directions and the elements. Jalaja Bonheim captures well the role of the Priestess, saying, "Today I would describe a priestess as a woman who lives in two worlds at once, who perceives life on earth against the backdrop of a vast, timeless reality. Whether or not she is mated to a human partner, she is a woman in love, wedded to being, to life, to love itself. Having offered herself, body and soul, in service of spirit, she mediates between matter and spirit, between the human and divine realms." [28]

The Priestess is the part of us that never dies, the wellspring of eternal wisdom that resides within each of us. She is our inner voice that arises with clear guidance and loving compassion; the voice that sings to us when we are quiet and connected to all that is. As the Priestess, we have many guides now; we have worked through the deeper obstacles in our path as a woman; we have learned to transform our fear of the dark into the power of night. In this chapter we work with Isis, the Great Mother and Queen of the World, who is able to transmute poison into power and reclaim her wisdom of the sacred feminine using the power of sacred sound.

The wise Priestess connects us to the vast spaciousness of the sacred feminine, honoring not only the earth but the sky as well. Many traditions honor the sky as father, aspects of the sacred masculine, connected to the qualities of transcendence, including the ceremonies in this book. I invite you to also reflect on the qualities of the sacred feminine that are akin to sky, celestial bodies, the starry night, the moon shining brilliantly, and the vastness of the cosmos. We hold the wise space of our own wombs within and contemplating the inner creative spaciousness helps to activate the Priestess.

---

28. Jalaja Bonheim, *Aphrodite's Daughters*, p. 18.

At this point on the path we have a clear understanding of our power and love in the shape of a woman. Our connection to the sacred feminine is clear and strong. Our inner Priestess urges us to begin sharing these gifts with others, to open ourselves up to become a channel for the community. The Priestess asks us to literally priestess—to hold space for ceremonies that honor the earth, love relationships, births, menses, and death. Connecting with not only the earth, but with other humans through art, dance, creating businesses, social networking, and political activism is a powerful part of Priestess work; she is our outward expression to the world. When we fully activate our inner Priestess, we become the goddess herself.

Cultivating Intuition

Beginning to work with and trust our intuition is crucial to activating our inner Priestess. Intuition is the inner wisdom within and guides us to follow our heart-body-mind connection that is in alignment with divine flow. When we tap into our intuition, we have a clearer sense of what we really want in our lives and are better able to trust the way that will unfold.

Learning to cultivate, listen, and act on intuition may take some practice. In ancient times, intuition was a very strong part of existence and aided hunters in tracking animals for food, clothing, and shelter. Intuition was used to speak directly with plants and know how they could be used for food and healing. Dr. Mona Lisa Schulz, a specialist in women's bodies, points out that "Intuition is a natural product of your brain and body…if you have a brain and a body and you sleep at night, by definition, you have all the equipment you need to be intuitive.…In fact, the areas of your feminine brain and body that make you unique—whether you have an exceptional

talent or are challenged by depression, anxiety, or other health problems—are exactly where to look to find your intuition."[29]

As we begin to uncover our intuitive side, we should remember that some people are very visual, while others perceive the world
through sound or touch, and this will translate directly into how
we intuit the world around us. Various ways to explore the intuitive part of our brain include: spending time in nature; creating art
through painting or sculpting; working with symbols and divination such as runes, tarot, or scrying; practicing meditation, yoga, or
tai chi; drumming and doing drum journeys; working with healing
arts such as Reiki or chakra healing.

One of the aspects of the Priestess is her role and function as
a seer or prophetess. By working with an oracle, you can develop
your intuition more keenly. I encourage you to seek out a particular oracle such as the tarot, runes, the I Ching, or other divination
method and begin to practice. To become effective at this kind of
work takes practice, and doing so is good for cultivating discipline,
working with symbolism, and understanding the patterns of life.
I recommend choosing only one deck or system to start with, and
really spending a few years working with that one until you have
mastered it. A good way to practice this is to choose one tarot deck,
pull a card each day, and then observe the day and how it unfolds
in relation to the card. I have worked primarily with one tarot, the
Aleister Crowley Thoth deck, for over a decade and found it useful in gaining better understanding in complex situations. There are
countless resources on these systems of divination, some listed at
the back of this book. We can also use nature as an invaluable tool
to hone our intuitive process. We each contain the wisdom of the
Priestess within; by using the exercise below, you can develop this
much more fully.

---

29.   Mona Lisa Schulz, M.D., *The New Feminine Brain*, p. 8.

Using Nature to Develop Your Intuition

Your inner Priestess is deeply in tune with her intuitive side, inspired by the natural world. To develop your intuition further, choose a place in nature that you enjoy. Pick one spot to work with for a three-month period. This will allow you to really come to know this particular place and allow it to speak to you. Be mindful that you will want to try and sit in this place regardless of rain or even snow. Make sure there is some level of comfort and that you will be warm (or cool) enough to do your work well. If it does pour rain on your session, do your best to stay, or retreat to a nearby covered area and watch from there. If there is really no place at all in nature you can get to, try to find a place you can visit outside your home: a rooftop, a sidewalk bench, any outdoor place that you can visit for a period of time that is not in your own space. Commit to the three months, marking it on your calendar. Buy a new journal or use one you already work with that has plenty of space for your notes, drawings, and intuitive workings.

Next, each morning when you wake up, set the intention, "I am listening to my intuitive self." Intention is very important when you begin working with the intuitive realms and energy. You may want to write down this affirmation, or one similar, and pin it up in your house to remind you throughout the day that you are honoring your intuition. Also state this intention (or something similar) every evening before sleep. Many powerful messages come from our dreams, and when we are clearly intending to hear those messages they will become more prominent. During this three-month time span, be sure to track the moons and your monthly cycle if you have not gone through menopause. This will give you more insight as to when your intuition is stronger. Several Native American traditions considered menses to be an extrasensory time of the month when women would retreat to the Moon Lodge to receive a vision.

Spend at least one session per week at your special place in nature. During the first month, simply receive. Go to your spot, create a sacred circle, give an offering to the nature spirits there. Make it simple if it is in a more public area so as to not draw much attention and simply observe. Note down the date, the moon cycle, and your own menses cycle for that day. Then sit quietly without writing. Allow thoughts to come and go, but do not make a strong effort to do any particular meditation. If you find you are thinking furiously, come back to your intention: "I am listening to my intuitive self." This practice not only opens up the intuitive and creative aspects of your being, it also disciplines you to become more focused. So often we receive a new practice from a teacher or friend or book and rush to try it, only to give up a week or so later because our mind becomes bored with it. If we can learn to tap more deeply into the intuitive self, boredom dissolves as each moment becomes wondrous and new. This is a good way to more fully activate our inner Priestess and enables us to use guidance when we begin to hold ceremony for others. Sit for at least twenty minutes. Notice the smells, the sounds, the colors of the sky, the grass, any flowers or trees, any other people passing by, the clouds. Do not write during this time; just be there with the place.

After twenty or thirty minutes, write down what comes to mind in a page or two in your journal. The first month, you can write anything down but keep it to a couple of pages. You may want to use colors to draw spontaneous images and/or draw with your nondominant hand. Often this can reveal certain qualities or messages. Do not analyze or try to understand what you are drawing or why.

During the second month, you are to come up with a question, a specific issue that is bothering you. Avoid yes or no questions; instead start the question with "how." You may want to ask about a relationship, a job, or a health problem. Ask in a way that leaves room for answers. For example, instead of asking, "What is my next career move?" try "How can I financially support myself in a way that fulfills my soul?" Follow the same practice you had for the first month, but ask your question aloud or in your mind after you have created the sacred circle and given an offering. Again, like before, observe the natural world around you, open and close your eyes as you feel inclined to, and try not to analyze what comes to mind. Simply allow the intuitive self to work around the issue. The world is a direct reflection of you and your being. If your question is clear, eventually a clear answer will come. Stick with the same question for at least two weeks; if you feel you have a clear answer, you may ask another question the second two weeks of the month. Giving the question those two different times to work with your intuition is more powerful than just once. Remember that by sitting in the sacred space and asking the question there, you are opening yourself up to receiving information that will often come in the form of omens, dreams, and synchronicities.

The last month is the same as the second, but you will ask a question for a family member or friend. This helps to cultivate the seer aspect of the inner Priestess. After the first two months (and only then), you can tell someone you trust what you have been doing. It is important to be quiet about your practice before this, as this helps to hold your power so it won't dissipate or lose ground. Choose a friend or family member whom you feel comfortable sharing this with and ask them to tell you an issue for you to work on. Repeat the sitting process, asking the question with your friend's name spoken or said in your mind. Sit for the twenty or thirty minutes, then write and draw. Again, look for omens or synchronicities as the weeks go by. Allow yourself to come to an answer after two weeks and give your friend the message. Repeat this with another friend (or the same one) using a different question for the last two weeks. In your final session, perform a simple gratitude ceremony to the place where you have been working, to thank the spirits for nourishing you during the three months. Of course you may continue to use this place for your intuitive work.

After you have finished your three-month work, this process can also be done in a very short time as well. You can practice this over the course of a weekend, taking the first morning to observe, the afternoon to ask your questions. I find it extremely valuable to first give yourself the longer span of time and commitment to the discipline to become very effective at the work before doing it more quickly. Allowing time to work in your life enhances the quality of your connectedness to the earth. We are often moving very fast, mentally, without really processing or integrating the massive sensory stimulus we receive. This practice enables us to slow down, hone our intuition, and learn about setting clear intentions for what we want. This becomes a valuable tool when activating the wisdom of the inner Priestess.

Isis

Isis, whose name means "great throne," is one of the longest worshipped goddesses in the world and is an all-encompassing aspect of the sacred feminine: a true priestess and Queen of the World. She was known as the Great Mother and connected to the moon. She is believed by some to be the origin of the Black Madonna and is connected to the dark mother, our distant ancestor who has evolved through time. She is linked to the Tree of Life, immortality and known to be the goddess of life-giving waters, the star goddess Sirius as well as the fertile pig goddess. Isis was in existence long before her stories were written down around 2500 BCE and was still held as a powerful female principle by Plutarch in the second century.

Of all the Egyptian goddesses, Isis reveals some of the most personal and human-like qualities, such as pain, grief, and anguish. She was continuously honored during the centuries of slow shift from the millennia of goddess worship into the cultivation of a priestly patriarch, and we see these messages reverberating in her stories. In one myth, Isis mourns her lost lover, Osiris, who is torn to pieces by his evil brother, Set. Isis reassembles Osiris except for his penis, makes love to him with a golden phallus in its place, and is impregnated with their son, the hawk-headed Horus. In the following, more ancient, and shorter myth below, Isis reclaims some of her own rightful power from the god Ra. Both of these stories illuminate the power of the Priestess that still resided in women in ancient times—a power that is rightfully ours and is becoming more accessible each day.

A Tale of Isis: Power of the Word

Isis was a beautiful woman who possessed words of power, but she was tired of men. Instead, she was fascinated with the realms of the gods, and even more, she had a strong desire to connect deeply with the realm of the spirits. One evening, she meditated in her heart, saying, "I too want to leave this earthly realm and become a goddess of like rank and power to Ra, god of the heavens."

Ra had grown old and weak. He dribbled and his spit fell to the earth. Isis took some of the spit and kneaded it with her magic to create a sacred serpent. Then she let the snake loose on the ground in front of Ra. As he walked down his path, the serpent bit him. He cried aloud, and the poison spread quickly throughout his body. "Who could possibly have done this to me? I am the all-powerful Ra! I am the god who has endless names and forms. I dwell deep within every god and no one—mortal or god—may infect me in such a way!" Nonetheless Ra remained stricken with the pain of the poison.

The children of every god came to him, grieving and weeping over his pain. Isis also came, bringing her words of magical power, and her mouth was full of the life breath. Isis was long known for her healing talismans. She was also capable of breathing life into the dead.

"I will heal you," she said, "but first, tell me your name, holy Father, for whatever it is that you name aloud will then be healed and live."

And Ra said, "I have made all things. I made the heavens above us. I made the earth, seas, the mountains, the trees, and the skies. I open my eyes and the light comes. I close my eyes and the darkness comes."

Isis said, "Still, you have not spoken your name aloud. Tell it to me and the poison will go."

The poison burned Ra like fire and he was in great pain. Finally, the great god agreed and said, "I consent, then. Isis, you may look within and my own name will pass from me into you." She looked within and found his name.

Isis called out, "Poison, leave Ra now! Let Ra live and the poison will die." These are the words of Isis, the mighty lady, the mistress of the gods, who knew Ra by his own name. Thus Isis healed Ra of the infliction she had put into him and herself became a goddess, full of wise power and immense love for the vast realms of the universe.

Keys to the Tale

This story begins with Isis feeling weary in her dealings with men and even gods. She wishes to connect more deeply with the spirit realms. The inner Priestess reflects our own yearning to more deeply connect with our spiritual selves and activates the fiery burning desire to become goddess. Ra has grown very old and is retiring. We can apply this also to our own world; the patriarch is indeed becoming tiresome! He is the part of us that, in previous stories, attempted to usurp our power, love, and wisdom as women. He is the voice of society that has become feeble in its attempt to prevent woman from working her mysterious magic. By her own craftiness,

Isis claims her status as a goddess, just as we can open to become a true Priestess of wisdom.

Isis takes some of Ra's spit and kneads it into a snake. She tricks him by using his fluids with her magic to create change so that she can become a goddess. This is akin to the work of an alchemist, the ability to transmute poison into bliss. Isis turns the spit into something that is both poisonous and sacred, a serpent, which is a potent symbol of the sacred feminine. The serpent signifies transition, transmutation, and a shift from one realm into another. It is an eternal, magical symbol, one that is distinctly connected to the sacred feminine, sexuality, birth, and rebirth. Myths all over the world speak of serpents as creators long associated with the sacred feminine. These serpents are a reflection of deep earth wisdom that is capable of imbuing people with magical abilities. In fact, according to Sjöö and Mor, there is a "world wide occurrence of the Goddess and her Serpent...[and] we can see the profound power as well as universality of this cosmological symbol, its range of endurance in the human mind."[30] The serpent's coiling nature and ancient connection to primordial life has in recent times been linked with DNA, the life-giving codes of our cells. Eve was offered the knowledge from the Tree of Life by a serpent. In India, Tantric practitioners carved snakes in their temples, shown coming out of women's vaginas, representing the vital life force and power of the sacred feminine. The serpent symbolizes our own inner ability to deeply transmute that which no longer serves us into the brilliant, powerful, loving wisdom of the Priestess. This is a magic that cannot be shaken, once achieved. When we give birth, experience death, raise children, we continuously make magic by using the old to create new.

Isis forms Ra's own bodily fluids into the serpent, which then bites him, sending poison through his body and blood. As a priest-

---

30. Sjöö and Mor, p. 58.

ess, Isis takes power into her own hands and compels the power and magic of the gods, determining her own destiny, rather than leaving it up to others. The snake is also a symbol of regeneration and cycles. Serpents shed their skin to make room for the new. Ra represents the part of us that has held on to the old way of creating power, a way that is dominant and no longer serves us. This aspect of our being wishes to keep old identities alive while our inner Priestess is working her wise magic to transmute them into an even more powerful woman. We have a choice—we can never give that incredible wise woman the chance to emerge and stay in our old patterns of ego, lower thinking, internalized pain, or we can choose to change and become even more powerful than we thought possible. Often times this scares us because becoming a wise woman means living from a place of courage and fearlessness. If we think of all the goddesses in this book, we see beings that are acting from a place of fiery power, love, and wisdom, clearly holding the ability to transmute and transform, even at the expense of not following all the rules, not always being nice, not doing things because we're supposed to, but doing them to dream a big vision into reality. Thus, relinquishing his name, Ra reflects the leap of faith we must take to grow ourselves into goddesses.

Ra's pain can be relieved by Isis and her healing abilities only if he reveals his name. He protests, claiming that he is the god of all things, all the earth and skies. Yet, long before Ra, many of these qualities were attributed to the goddess of the Paleolithic and Neolithic times, when the mother was revered for thousands of years. Isis inspires us to use our own cleverness to reclaim what is rightfully ours. Women have the right to create the kind of life that nourishes our well-being; we have the right to have the kind of birth that supports our bodies and our babies; we have the right to leave a relationship that no longer fulfills us; we have the right to be both sexual and spiritual; we have the right to call out to the winds and honor the spirits; we have the right to imbue every day with wisdom—feminine wisdom that is intuitive, cyclical, clear, and brilliant, even if our society says otherwise. We have the right to dance wildly in the woods, to take back the night from those who would crush the feminine in their own ignorance and pain. As our inner Priestess is activated, we must continuously seek out ways to make magic, make love, make the earth anew.

This myth also illuminates the power of the spoken word that is a crucial quality of the Priestess. The power of the spoken word is a part of every culture, religion, and ceremony throughout the world. In the ancient Vedas of India, certain yogic techniques consist of mantras or sacred sounds that are spoken to activate the chakras, with the voice being the carrier of that activation. In Sanskrit, each letter is believed to be sacred, and many are considered bija or seed syllables, which when spoken correctly will activate certain areas of the energetic body. Similarly, in South American, African, Native American, and Tibetan cultures, specific sounds are used to call on the spirits. Chants are passed down orally through the generations and guarded by the shamans or spirit keepers of a tradition so as not to tamper with or dissolve the potency of the sacred sounds.

Using the power of words and sacred sound, we activate our inner Priestess, opening up the way for higher wisdom in our daily lives.

EXERCISE 8.2

Using Sacred Sound

This exercise encourages you to use sacred sound in different aspects of your life. First, choose a sacred sound and practice working it during your daily meditation. You may know a mantra given to you by a teacher or you can use something simple such as Aum sound. Spend a few minutes during your meditative practice chanting the sound and if possible, visualizing the symbol. Notice the affect the sound work has on your body and mind.

You may choose to incorporate sound into your ritual and ceremony work as well. When you set any intention, use your voice to ask for what you want. Call out to the spirits and universe with your request. When you voice aloud what you want, it becomes much clearer to yourself as well as your guides what you are asking for. For example, during the full moon ceremony, instead of simply making a list of your intentions, call them out aloud. Keep it simple and clear, and your ability to manifest will become much stronger.

Another way to work with sacred sound is to discover a dream song. You can do this in combination with the intuition exercise above. Spend one of the times in your power spot asking for a song. This requires you to move around in different areas of your spot. Take paper and pen and sit in your sacred spot. Ask for a song, harmony, line, word, or sacred sound from that spot. Each place in nature has its own vibration, song, or tone. Then simply listen and wait for the song or tone to be revealed to you. Once you hear it, write it down. Then move to another area near or around your sacred spot. Again, be quiet and listen and wait for the song or tone. It may come simply as a word, a color, a feeling, or an image. Write down whatever you experience. Repeat this in five or more spots within your sacred area and then put the images, phrases, tones, or colors together to create a song. Even if you are not musical at all, this will work, because your intention is clear. This song becomes a personal wisdom song and can be used in your Priestess work.

Sky Journey

In ancient Egypt, Nut was the goddess of the skies who swallowed the sun every evening and gave birth to it each morning. Even today, our name for the galaxy, the Milky Way, is rooted in the sacred feminine. In several worldwide myths, this stream of stars was the milky river of the great mother goddess's breasts, a beautiful image that invokes nourishment from our skies. By honoring the sacred feminine in the form of the sky, we are connecting with our vast self, our star-like qualities of brilliance, beauty, and expansiveness. In this journey, you will travel to the upper realms to connect with your inner Priestess.

Gather together the following items:

- Four candles and offerings for the four directions
- A large silver candle for the sky realms or milky way
- An offering of copal or other resin (such as frankincense) that can be burned in a small clay bowl
- Pictures of space, the cosmos, star nurseries, the Milky Way, or any celestial images of heavens
- A drum or drumming CD, or other repetitive sound maker
- A journal and pen

Before you begin, think of a place where you can imagine leaving to enter the sky, such as a mountain or cliff top or the top of some trees. Next, call in the four main directions, light the candles, and make your offerings. Also call in the directions of above, below, and center, but do not assign them as father sky and mother earth. Create sacred space. Then call in the feminine sky realms, intending guidance from the starry realms in the guise of the sacred feminine. Light the silver candle and give the offering of copal or frankincense by burning it in the clay bowl.

Set your intention to journey to the upper realms to meet your inner Priestess. Lie down and cover your eyes. In your mind, restate your intention, such as, "I intend to visit the sky realms to meet my inner Priestess." Begin your drumming CD, or if you are doing this in a group and have a drummer present, have the person begin to drum a steady beat. Imagine yourself on the top of the mountain or cliff. Visualize yourself leaving the mountain top and moving upward into the sky. Imagine that you pass through a door or barrier and into the celestial realms. As the drumming continues, let yourself move through the realms, exploring and stating your intention.

Eventually your inner Priestess will appear. She may be in the form of an animal, bird, human teacher, or even light. Be open to any messages or information she has in order to help you activate the inner Priestess in your daily life. After twenty to thirty minutes, the drummer can begin to slow down the beat. Imagine coming back down from the skies or upper realms, through the door, back into your body. Thank the guides as needed and remember the wisdom given to you. When the drumming stops, slowly stretch and sit up.

Write down what you have been told so that you can further use the knowledge. Watch for dreams and omens that speak of synchronicity in connection with your journey to the celestial realms. You can revisit this realm anytime.

When you are finished, dissolve the sacred space by snuffing the sky candle and thanking the feminine skies. Release the four directions and also snuff those candles as well.

Creating Your Own Ceremony

Cultivating our inner Priestess asks us to more fully become a community participant, whether this involves networking with friends or leading community events. The Priestess has a clear sense of her gifts and knows how to pass them on to help others. She knows exactly what she is capable of, which tools to use and when, and also when to delegate tasks to others. Connecting with the earth and people through art, dance, creating businesses, social networking, or political activism is a powerful part of Priestess work; she is our outward expression to the world. She is the gift we choose to give back because of what we have overcome.

I encourage you to sit with all the skills you have learned thus far and create a ceremony for a group of people. This may be a full moon ceremony, as in Chapter Five, or ceremony to reclaim menarche, as in Chapter Two, or a different kind of ceremony altogether. Design a ceremony that feels appropriate for you; it can be something very simple, such as taking a group of people to a nice spot in nature and creating a circle of intention. When we branch out and expand ourselves, we dissolve the attachment to our lower ego-self and open up to the broad-reaching pulse of universal wisdom. This helps us bring our power and love into a place of wisdom, where we begin to share our work with others.

nine

THE CRONE
Dissolving the Forms

What is life? It is the flash of a firefly in the night.
It is the breath of a buffalo in the winter time.
It is the little shadow which runs across the grass
and loses itself in the sunset.
—CROWFOOT, APRIL 1890, ON HIS DEATHBED

Imagine you are sitting quietly, connected in to the energy
of the earth. Its living wisdom pulses through you. You sit
with the knowing that as all things are born, all things die;
nothing stays the same. Yet your heart is open and full of
love, your body imbued with power and your being with
wisdom. As you sit in quiet contemplation, visualize an old
woman coming toward you. She is the Crone. She emanates
the most powerful, yet loving force you have ever felt. She is
the earth herself and the keeper of all the stories that have

ever been told. She holds a gift for you in her hand. You bow
to her in greeting and open your hands to receive her gift.
Notice what this gift is and remember, because this will help
you as you work through the many changes that life inevita-
bly brings. This is the wisdom of death and endings.

The final stage of our journey brings us full circle to the ancient, elder Crone. Here the wisdom of the sacred feminine lies in the process of releasing and letting go, in the form of endings, darkness, deep rest. The Crone is the archetype of decay, destruction, and death. She resides in the darkest hours of the night, in the hollows of trees, in the depths of the deepest oceans, in the ground as decaying, rotting flesh. The word *Crone* is similar to the Greek word *chronos*, the awareness of time. The Crone holds the relentless reminder that all creatures and living things on this earth are timebound, that we each reside in a form that is decaying and dying. According to Barbara Walker, "The 'Crone' may have descended from Rhea Kronia as Mother of Time, though the title has been linked with Coronis, the carrion crow, since crows and other black creatures were sacred to the Death goddess."[31] There is an incredible freedom in this reality, and with her dark rattles and crackling bones, the Crone smiles gleefully, sparking our hearts to not take anything too seriously. All things that rise must also fall away.

The Crone is our guide during the aging process, the physical wrinkling of our skin and the graying of our hair. At the time of menopause, the time of crossing over into the elder years, we are first visited by the Crone. As Demetra George remarks, this is the stage "when a woman begins to reap the harvest of wisdom that arises from all her varied life experiences."[32] This may also occur in

---

31. Barbara Walker, *The Woman's Encyclopedia of Myths and Secrets*, from the entry "Crone," p. 187.

32. Demetra George, *Mysteries of the Dark Moon*, p. 221.

younger women during times of illness, spiritual or personal crises, depression, death of a family member, divorce, or change in career. I felt the Crone powerfully in my life when I had cancer at nineteen. Losing all my hair and going through chemotherapy was a kind of death process and resulted in a rebirth, transitioning from young adult to a woman who had faced her own mortality. Similarly, when my newborn daughter died, the mantra that "death is the matrix for rebirth" resounded in my mind and kept me afloat during those very dark days.

The Crone is the one who sits with us each time we bleed, as this is a small death. She guides us when we cross over into menopause, and she is there when we leave this body and earth. The sacred feminine is found within these powerful transitions and holds the knowledge of death as well as the power of rebirth. She is the compost for fertile ground, the destructive fires that burn away to allow for new growth, the ashes from which the beginnings of life will stir once again. The Crone brings us full circle, uniting with the Fire Bearer to revisit the void, the place of darkness, the earth that lays fallow, ready for new seeds and embers. We find the Crone in the form of Grandmother Corn in the Cherokee myth below. She embodies the death process and is reborn as corn, the food that will continue to nourish her people.

The Dying Process

The Crone is distinctly connected with the dying as well as the dead. When we find ourselves in times of despair, illness, sorrow, and loss, it is the Crone who reminds us of the power and wisdom found within these intense moments. She gives us the opportunity to practice our compassion with those who are leaving this form and moving into another. Death is similar to birth in that it is a transition time. Honoring this time is crucial and should be deeply respected and treasured, just as birth should be, although this is often not the case. The Crone is our reminder that diamond-brilliant insight and crystalline vision of clarity can emerge when we are around those who are dying. If we can approach this process with love and acceptance, rather than worry and anxiety, we may be able to tap into the real message that is borne by the Crone, the message that all things change form.

In our culture, we have an abnormally strong fear of dying. We spend billions of dollars to maintain a young-looking face and body and to wear youthful fashions. We do not deal well with people who are sick, terminally ill, dying, or dead. In stark contrast, in places such as India the ill and the dying live with the family, and everyone is both a witness and a participant in the very real process of decay and death. When the person dies, as our neighbor did while we lived in South India, the response is astonishing. Our neighbor, an elderly man who had a heart attack in the night, was someone we interacted with most days. His grandchildren played with our child, their chickens wandered into our garden occasionally, we helped them rent rooms during high tourist season, and so on.

We awoke one morning to hear women wailing and crying. This carried on for hours, and we were told that he had passed away. Much of the work ceased in the village as people began to come and pay respects: the milkman stopped selling milk for a while, laborers stopped working, women ceased washing. Streams of people began to flow down our small lane to their house, along with an amazing amount of food that seemed to appear out of nowhere. Songs were sung, food shared, and oil lamps burned continuously over the course of three days. When the son had arrived and the ceremonies had been performed, they built a giant fire right in their front yard and put the deceased grandfather/father/husband there and watched him burn. The smoke swirled up into the air as everyone participated in the transformation of body to ash. Hindus believe strongly in reincarnation, and some of their prayers were for this soul to find a good rebirth—prayers for the return of positive kar-

mic influences so that he would be born more aware, more conscious, and perhaps a bit closer to true enlightenment.

In Kerala (South India), when a body has turned completely to
ash, some of the ashes are buried right there, on the property, and
the rest is kept aside to be put into the ocean on the appropriate
day. We lived at the beach where, each year, Keralites brought the
ashes of dead ancestors and floated them into the waves. This is a
joyous occasion filled with much celebration, dance, music, and fes-
tivity that continues on late into the night for an entire week. After
our neighbor's ashes were buried in the yard, his family marked the
spot and planted a new coconut tree on top. Kerala lawns and gardens are dotted with the white stones and palms marking the burial
spots of their beloved relatives. This process inspires us to reconnect with our own ancestors and recognize the reality that our bodies are intimately connected to the earth.

Kinds of Death

There are many kinds of death. It is so important, so inherently crucial, to understand that all things that are born will die; that is the
very nature of the universe, our world, our mind. When we begin to
really glimpse this and see through it, we come to a kind of clarity,
even a feeling of relief. We suddenly don't have to take everything
so seriously; the house does not have to be perfect, the outfit amazing, the work impeccable. All things rise and fall away, and perhaps
the less we plan or try to make things a certain way, the more naturally they will come together and then dissolve. Our culture has
burgeoned into a mass of consumer culture, a corporate governance
in which the end profit is the only goal. When we consume on this
level, and create without the proper balance of death and decay, our
overuse turns toxic, just as our world is now teeming with toxicity,
extinctions, polluted air and water. When we live from a place of

wisdom and fearlessness, we recognize death as an advisor and can live a more balanced life.

Finding and honoring our quiet side, our deeper, darker side, the part of us that lays fallow brings us closer to wholeness. If we can connect with death before it is imposed by external failures, we will be better able to deal with things *as they are*. We will not feel traumatized by the incessant changes that life brings and the cycles of waxing and waning that our bodies, souls, and minds naturally go through. We face many types of deaths: every day the sun sets and the day dies; the morning brings the death of night; the cup of tea is emptied; species become extinct. At my Zen center, we would sit and contemplate how each inhalation actually kills thousands of microorganisms, acknowledging that indeed we are death bringers. We do not have to be afraid of death. The contemplation of death and impermanence is one of the most powerful teachings of the Crone. She is the part of the sacred feminine that not only represents death, but illuminates the wisdom of endings, giving birth to new beginnings.

EXERCISE 9.1

Envisioning Your Death

The reality of death is a potent opportunity for contemplation, to simply sit and be with the realization that not only will we die, but all of those around us will die. The rocks and stones and trees will go on for much longer than us; even our houses and cars will probably outlive our temporal existence. This exercise helps you connect to the beautiful realization that you are a part of the infinite universe. You can use this exercise several times a year, at your menstruation times, or when you cross over into menopause.

Sit in a meditative position and imagine that you have died and left the earth. Imagine your funeral and who will visit you, who will weep over your loss. Then imagine life continuing on without you. Imagine your immediate family dealing with the loss and then beginning to move on, into new phases and ways of being without your presence. Visualize your job without you being there, the company carrying on. Visualize the circle of women who grieve over you but also celebrate your return to spirit. See the world and its continuation without you in this present form. Imagine parties or gatherings that you would usually attend going on without you; classes held with new teachers and students; connections being reformed and people growing in new and different ways. Notice how this makes you feel. Do you feel lighter, less important? It may feel good to realize that you don't have to take yourself so seriously, that in your death life will continue on without you. It always has and always will! How light and effortless you can be in your life, knowing that perhaps there is not so much difference whether you are here or there, in this world or the next.

The following story captures the beauty of the Crone in her journey from elder and a place of wisdom to the power of rebirth. Numerous stories around the world tell the story of a god or goddess turning into a sacred tree or plant. This story comes from the Native American Cherokee tribe and tells the story of how corn was given to the people. It illustrates the qualities of rebirth, one of the central aspects of the Crone. Through the death of the grandmother, corn and the ability to feed the people are born.

The Coming of Corn[33]

Long ago, when the world was very new, an old woman lived with her grandson. They lived a quiet and happy life until the boy was seven years old. Then his grandmother gave him his first bow and

---

33.   This story by Joseph Bruchac is reprinted here with his permission from the following source: Michael J. Caduto and Joseph Bruchac, *Keepers of the Earth: Native American Stories and Environmental Activities for Children.* Golden, CO: Fulcrum, 1989.

arrow. Excited, he went out to hunt for game and brought back a small bird.

The grandmother was delighted and remarked, "Ah, you will be a great hunter one day. Let us celebrate this moment with a feast." She disappeared behind the cabin and went into a small storehouse. She came back out with her basket full of dried corn and made a delicious soup from the bird and the corn.

From then on, the boy hunted every day. He brought back something each day, and the grandmother went into the storehouse, brought out corn and made soup. One day, when the grandmother wasn't looking, the boy peered curiously into the storehouse. To his surprise, the storehouse was empty! Yet that evening, when he brought back his game for her to cook, she again returned to the storehouse and came out with her basket full of dry corn.

"How strange," the boy said to himself. "I will find out what is happening."

The next day, he brought back a bird and waited for his grandmother to go out to the storehouse. This time he followed her into the storehouse and peered between the logs. There he saw a very peculiar thing happen. The storehouse was completely empty, yet his grandmother leaned over the basket and began to rub her body. As she smoothed her hands down the sides of her body, corn sprouted from her flesh, appearing through her clothes like magic. The dry corn fell into the basket and filled it up. The boy grew afraid. What if she was a witch? He silently stole back to the house to wait. The grandmother returned and saw the look on her grandson's face.

"Grandson," she said, "you followed me to the storehouse and saw what I did there."

"Yes, grandmother," said the boy.

The old woman shook her head in sorrow. "Dear grandson, then I must leave you now," she said, her eyes filling with tears. "Now that you know my secret, I can no longer live as I did before.

Tomorrow, before the sun rises, I shall be dead. Now, you must do as I tell you and then you will feed the people once I am gone."

The old woman looked very weary. The boy moved to sit closer to her, but she waved him away. "You cannot help me now, grandson. Just do as I tell you. Once I have died, clear away a patch of ground on the south side of our lodge. This is the place where the sun is the strongest and the brightest. Make sure the earth is completely bare. Once you have done that, drag my body over the ground seven times and then bury me deep in that bright earth. Then you must keep the ground clear. If you do as I say, I promise you that you will see me again and you will also be able to feed the people." Then the old woman grew very quiet. Silence hung in the air as she closed her eyes one last time. Before morning came, she died.

Her grandson followed her words exactly. He cleared away the sunniest spot on the south side of their lodge. It took a long time, for there were many trees, tangled vines, and deeply rooted plants. Finally the earth was completely cleared and bare, ready for his grandmother. He carefully dragged her body across the earth. Wherever a drop of her blood fell onto the barren earth, a small plant sprouted. After he dragged it seven times across, many plants had poked through the surface of the cleared land. Then he buried her deeply, laying her body to rest one final time. As time passed, the grandson diligently kept the ground clear around the small plants. As they grew taller, he heard the whispering of his grandmother's voice through the leaves. The days grew longer and brighter, and the plants grew taller and stronger. When the plants were as tall as a person, they grew long tassels at the top of their stalks. The long, fine strands reminded the boy of his grandmother's hair. Finally, ears of corn formed on each plant and, just as his grandmother promised, the boy was able to take the corn and feed the people. Although the grandmother was gone from the earth as she had once been, she was now with the people forever as corn.

Keys to the Tale

This is a simple story with only two characters; it is the story of a grandmother passing her legacy, her art, and her power to the later generation, to her grandson. Grandmothers have very special relationships with their grandchildren. Often the connection that grandparents and grandchildren have bypasses the karma that is so strong between parents and children, and there is a bridge that connects them across the generations. Grandparents hold gifts and precious stories to be passed down to their grandchildren. In our society, we have very little respect for those who are old. We need to be reminded of the inherent wisdom that grows alongside a person's earth path. Try to remember some of the gifts and wisdom that have been shared by your own grandmothers and grandfathers.

The grandmother represents our inner wisdom and sacred feminine connection to the earth. Our bodies bleed each month, give birth, and die, which links us directly with the cycles of time and life, death and rebirth. The grandmother is also a symbol of a cycle that is dying out, while the boy represents new growth, a new project, a new cycle of life, a birth.

The young boy spies on his grandmother and witnesses her secret magic. To his surprise, he finds that his grandmother is not collecting corn from a storage place, but is actually able to create dried corn from her body. This is a powerful gift of the sacred feminine, the ability to create nourishment from our own bodies. The grandmother is a Crone, an elder, and her magic comes in the form of creating food. This is found in many myths: the creation of certain plants, trees, and sacred medicine from the goddess's body parts. In Hawai'ian mythology, Hina, the multidimensional goddess of the moon, corals, and winds, leaves behind a piece of herself when she tires of her husband and her dirty children. She escapes to the moon, but as she flies up, her husband grabs her leg; it breaks off and turns into a sweet potato. To this day, the hau-lani sweet potato is named for the fleeing Hina. Our own bodies will die and return to the earth, able to create new life in other forms. The grandmother represents not only wisdom, but specifically earth wisdom, creative wisdom, and a kind of spiritual nourishment.

Once the grandson has witnessed his grandmother's power, then her role shifts entirely. This reveals another potent quality of the Crone: the keeper of magic and medicine. In order to hold a teaching deeply, one must sit with this teaching, this profundity, for many years and have the ability to not share it until it is ready. One of the most powerful teachings of Tibetan Buddhism is Chöd, a practice that was given to Machig Lapdrön, a woman of eleventh century Tibet. This practice is considered to be the most shamanic of the Tibetan practices because it involves the Crone-like wisdom of visualizing our bodies as offerings to our demons. Just as the grandmother in the story offers her body so that she may nourish the people, Chöd practitioners envision offering their body, cutting away limbs, head, brains, and organs in order to become full of compassionate wisdom. Giving the gift of her own body to nourish future generations is the most selfless practice the grandmother can do, and by witnessing her power, the grandson is able to help her bear fruit for his people. The Crone is the reminder that we too can become selfless and cultivate our own power and magic as a gift for future generations.

When the grandson has discovered his grandmother's secret, she begins to weep. She is sorrowful in her realization that she will now die, leaving this form to transition into another. Yet she knows there is nothing to be done and tells the boy that there is nothing he can do, that she will leave her body by the morning light. This is one of the most potent and clear wisdoms of the Crone: knowing when it is time to let go. If we can call that wisdom into our daily life, we have learned something that is crucial to the acceptance of real life. The sacred feminine works in cycles and circles, not in lines and squares. The Crone bears the message that all things come to an end, that death is the matrix for rebirth, that decay and compost are crucial for our soul's growth. The grandmother of the story knows this inherently and embraces the coming night as her time to let go and die.

The grandson becomes the one who carries out the message that she holds; he becomes the keeper of his grandmother's magic. In order to do this, he must complete a special task. As we have found so often in myth and stories, the completion of a task is crucial to the development of aspects of our psyche. This is the importance of dissolving the small self into the larger self—doing something that is bigger and greater than us, something that requires special attention and will help many people. Like the boy in this story, we may be given a certain talent or message that can be passed on to others.

Here the grandson symbolizes the holder of old knowledge as well as seeds for the gifts for his people. He represents the deepest, wisest part of us that knows the ancient magic of our ancestors and the way in which to share this magic. As we have progressed along the path of the sacred feminine, we have touched the rich power, love, and wisdom of our being and are now encouraged to share what we have learned.

The grandson does his task well, carefully clearing the patch of earth and dragging his grandmother's body across the earth seven times. This is a disturbing image in the story, the image of a young boy dragging his grandmother back and forth across a plot of freshly turned earth. It almost seems irreverent, yet shows how the body is certainly going to decay; what the boy needs now is not to look at her dead body but to use it. He needs the blood that was her life force to feed the soil, from which sprouts of corn will appear. Here, the wisdom of the Crone is again apparent, the crystal-clear reminder that we are short-lived in a temporal body, one that could be easily dragged to and fro, a body that does not go with us at death. We might ask ourselves, then: Have we lived, truly *lived*, a life that feels full upon death? How much time have we spent worrying, obsessing, pondering over things that are attached to this body? If we were to ask the Crone for her guiding wisdom, what might she say?

As the blood drops land on the earth, the new sprouts of corn pop up. This is the message of immanence, a message of the goddess, and is very much one of the crucial missing keys from our progress-oriented society. It cannot be emphasized enough how important it is to deeply contemplate the process of death and its transitioning into rebirth. Of course, it happens all around us, every single day, but we have become very clever at avoiding this reality until it smacks us in the face in the form of miscarriage, illness, a breakup, a death...or any kind of ending. Simply being with the process and allowing it to unfold is crucial to the next stage, the brilliant, creative stage of rebirth. The more we suppress and fight the decaying and death process, the harder it is to reach a place of new growth. It is simply a cycle of life, yet fighting that and trying to remain linear, against the natural ebb and flow of the universe, is like trying to stand up to the ocean or an earthquake! When we have a better grasp on accepting endings, we can carry out our task more clearly and use the death or ending to fertilize our new ground.

Finally, the corn grows up from the sprouts, and the boy witnesses his grandmother's voice, her hair, and her ears though the growing corn. As he tends his new plants, he is growing food that will nourish not only himself and his people, but the coming generations. He is nourished not only by the essence of his grandmother, but by the food that has grown up out of her body. We might ask ourselves what we have to give—not only to those around us, but what we might leave behind for future generations. The Crone, in her ancient wisdom of seeing the ages over a vast period of time, is deeply connected to the earth and knows how to leave something to help the people of earth. Few could say the same today in our culture. Thinking more deeply on the "long now," the vast expanse of time, we can connect with the past and future generations, our multidimensional selves, and the part of us that is much greater than this one small, temporal body.

Sitting with Death

This exercise is a practice of sitting with loved ones at death or during the dying process. It is a very simple exercise that calls for using mindfulness and being fully present in the moment. Simply sit with the person and hold their hand. Visualize your heart center meeting their heart center. Rest in the pace of their breathing, trying your best to allow it to be, without fear. If they are struggling for breath, be with that; if their breath is slow and shallow, experience that through them for several minutes.

If the person is cognizant, you may want to ask them if there is anything they want to say or express. Allow time for them to say it. This moment is an opportunity to deeply allow them to say what needs to be said without judgment or fear. They may choose to reminisce, tell stories of a deep past, or recall memories of long ago. Often the mind is struggling at this time, struggling to simply give up and let go. During this process, you will want to tend to their needs and help them feel as comfortable as possible. Sometimes people will recount things they have seen and heard during the night or during sleep, things that may not be there. Try not to dismiss the person's experiences; often when people are drifting into another world they experience aspects of the other realms. This is akin to experiences during dream time and astral travel.

This is also the time to let closure happen, in its own way, naturally. Perhaps the dying person has certain requests or may feel a measure of regret about certain things that happened in their life. Try to honor these requests or simply hold space for the mental and emotional processes that are happening. More importantly, try not to pressure the dying person into admitting something or create any kind of unnecessary stress during this sensitive time. When my grandfather was dying, I gave him Reiki several times and he often drifted into memories of the past and felt compelled to tell me things that had happened to him when he was young, things he loved about his life as well as events that he felt some regret about. I simply let him express these stories as he drifted in and out of consciousness.

When the moment of death comes, it may take some time for the breath to leave the body. Along with the breath, the spirit will drift out and onward into the next realm. As with birth, it is often better if the lights are low and there is little to no stress around the person at death. According to Tibetans, this process is subject to karmic winds and external forces that can affect our ability to navigate toward light and rebirth effectively. The more clear and lucid we are around the person at the time of death, the more easily the spirit will move into a place of calm, healing, and brilliance.

When the spirit leaves, many traditional cultures continue sitting with the body for some time. We do not usually have this option in the West. Yet, we can at the very least intend calm, beauty, and quietness as this process shifts into the practicalities of dealing with the body. Finally, when the body is cremated or buried, we can perform a ceremony to honor the spirit that was briefly in form in this lifetime on earth, intending it to find peace and harmony beyond.

Ceremony to Honor Menopause

This is a ceremony to support the passing over into the Crone years, the elder years, the time when blood is carried within. This is not the old, haggard Crone of the patriarch's demonizing, but a very vital, wisdom-bearing, and alive Crone. In fact, this word "haggard," which is often associated with Crone, originally applied to hawks and meant "untamed."[34] The Crone has died to a new way of being, allowing her energy to be transformed from a woman who has the ability to carry a new human life to a time when she carries other kinds of life in the form of projects, support for family and friends, and spiritual growth and development. The Native American tradition honored this transition as the time of "wise blood." Instead of pouring out each month, the blood is held within and the woman has now reached her wisdom years. This is the time when a woman has often fulfilled her worldly duties of caring for family and can now focus on her community as an elder as well as on her spiritual path.

This ceremony can be performed with a group of women: girls who have yet to experience menses, women who are currently having menses, and women who have undergone and passed through menopause. Including women at all stages of their life gives the younger women a chance to honor and respect the elders as they embrace their cronehood and wisdom years.

Gather together the following items:

- Pictures and images that show cronehood and speak of transitions, such as Hecate, the guardian of the crossroads, who helps souls move from death to rebirth, images of your grandmothers, or Changing Woman from the Navajo tradition
- Music and rhythm makers
- Four candles for the four directions, as well as candles for mother earth and father sky (and optional center)
- A foot bath with warm water
- A soothing oil such as lavender or rose
- Flower petals
- A threshold or gateway, such as an arch or netting decorated with long flowing ribbons and flowers
- Feathers

---

34. Mary Daly, *Gyn/ecology*, p. 15.

- Four small altar tables, each decorated with images and qualities of the four sacred elements: air in the east, fire in the south, water in the west, earth in the north

Before the ceremony, the younger women should create the space for the elder women. The girls who have not yet crossed over into menses can prepare the flower petals, filling up baskets with many flowers, and prepare the gateway, decorating it lovingly with ribbons, fabric, silks, and flowers. This will be the gateway or arch that symbolizes women who have passed into menopause, into the cronehood years.

The women who are still menstruating should prepare the five main altars. The altar creation can be an event in itself and should be infused with great joy and preparation to honor the elder women of the community. Mothers may be present, telling their daughters about the importance of honoring the grandmothers. Stories of their own grandmothers may be told as the preparation continues, to help the young women understand where they have come from and what paths have opened up because of the power, strength, courage, and wisdom of the elder women.

The five altars are:

- An altar for the Crone herself, with images of older women and crone goddesses both loving and fearsome
- An altar in the east for air, with items such as feathers, incense, a smudge stick, an image of sun rising
- An altar in the south for fire, with candles, copal, a cauldron, a snakeskin, images of lava and burning fires
- An altar in the west for water, with bowls of water, images of the setting sun
- An altar in the north for earth, with crystals, stones, bones, and images of the earth

A time is specified when the space will be ready for the crone women to arrive. They enter the space and are anointed with oil by the younger, non-menstruating girls. The girls wash the elders' feet, which is an ancient, time-honored tradition of respect. Once that has been done, and everyone is gathered together, one woman acting as priestess (an elder, a woman who has already passed into crone-hood) calls the seven directions as well as specifically invoking the goddess as crone and dark mother and asking for her guidance and blessings. Then each crone circuits the room and visits the altars at each direction while the women and girls sing.

As each woman visits the elemental altars, she might reflect on the gifts she has received in her life thus far from air (mind and breath), fire (spirit and transformation), water (emotions and cleansing), and earth (body and groundedness). Perhaps she gives an offering, such as a candle or some incense. Finally she joins the circle of singing women and adds her voice to the chant. When each woman has finished her circuitous visit to the altars, a space at the northern end of the circle is made for the women who now sym-bolically pass into their cronehood. Here the women sit, waiting to pass through the archway. The priestess calls for a time of silence and quiet, having the women contemplate the cycles of life and think of a time when something came to an end.

The priestess gives a large offering of copal to the cauldron, as a message to the spirits that the women are now to pass through the arch into cronehood. She begins singing a song, which can be joined in by the other women.

One by one, each crone is then taken by one of the women through the gateway at the center of the circle as a symbolic pass-ing into her cronehood. There she is met by the priestess and gives an offering to the altar of the Crone. This offering should be very specific, something that symbolizes what she is leaving behind as she enters cronehood. This is essential to the power of the ritual: to honor, let go, and release her time as mother/life-bearer (whether she had children or not). This can be a picture of her time as a mother, a symbol of the career she worked hard at, an image of a child, anything that represents the powerful creative times of her younger years when she bled with the rhythm of the moons. It may be something more symbolic as well, such as a representation of the full moon, a red cloth, or simply a beautiful flower.

After the crone gives the offering, the priestess then touches a dagger to her shoulders and head, symbolizing the power of cronehood, embraces her, and welcomes her to the wisdom years. The crone sits in the northern section of the circle and is given two shawls: one white and one black, symbols of the return to a time without bloods and a connection to the Crone.

Once all the crones have moved through the gateway into their cronehood, the song winds down into silence again. Then the girls who have not yet become women stand and pass before the crones, bowing their heads and leaving the circle. They are followed by the women who are still bleeding, leaving behind only the priestess and the crones, who now spread out and make their own small circle. The talking stick is passed around and each woman takes a turn expressing herself as a newly blessed crone, as an elder. She may want to state an intention for this new phase of her life or release a fear that she is holding on to. She may want to express her sorrow at the aging process or losing friends and family, as well as her excitement about retirement and pursuing new projects and ideas.

When this process is over, the crones then stand together and hold hands, powerfully calling in the intention to connect these women to this moment, that this is a seed of power and strength for later times when things become more difficult in the next phase of life. This should be led by the priestess, who burns a special kind of offering such as sweet grass or cedar to bless this intention. The priestess thanks and releases the directions, mother earth, father sky, and center, finally closing the circle. The women are bonded in sacred ribbons of light with each other, energetically as well as physically. They have symbolically entered into cronehood time together.

CONCLUSION

Every great dream begins with a dreamer.
Always remember, you have within you the strength,
the patience, and the passion to reach for the stars,
to change the world.
—HARRIET TUBMAN

This is a time like no other. We cannot go back to the dim past of the goddess and the grandmothers of culture, to a time that seems lost like the fading of sunset. None of us really know exactly where we came from, but we do know that we must evolve or die. The sacred feminine is one key, but so is the sacred masculine. We must recognize that we each, both individually and collectively, have the power to dream a different dream. We can dance the wonder of the universe in every form, in all its diversity. It seems we have no choice at this point. And so I encourage you: do not waste your life.

I conclude this book with a story from the Lakota nation of the Great Plains. This story is old, but it is new too; it is the story of a sacred woman who is bringing a message of truth and peace, a message that is sorely needed in today's world. It is a message of deep reverence: reverence for our mothers and fathers, our grandmothers and grandfathers, reverence for our children, and reverence for our dear Mother Earth. Long ago, White Buffalo Calf Woman brought the sacred pipe to the people, and I believe she is still bringing it, she is still carrying the story we so desperately need to hear. She carries the wisdom of our interconnectedness, and the ability to steward this incredible earth. She carries the power to walk with grace and strength even in the face of obstacles. She holds the deep well of love for all of our relations. It is my sincere hope that as we call in the power, love, and wisdom of the sacred feminine, we will find and use the medicine of White Buffalo Calf Woman to heal our planet.

The White Buffalo Calf Woman and the Sacred Pipe[35]

Two young men were sent out to scout for game, as it was a time when little food was available, and the people in the camp were hungry. The men set out on foot, as this was also the time before horses, the great Spirit Dogs, were given to the people. After a long time hunting with no luck, the two men climbed to the top of a hill and looked to the west.

"What is that?" asked one young man.

"I cannot tell, but it is coming toward us," said the other.

And it came toward them. At first it seemed to be an animal, but as the form came closer, they realized it was a woman. She was dressed in a white buffalo skin and carried something in her hands. She walked so lightly that it seemed as if she were barely walking at all, instead floating along the surface of the earth with her feet barely touching.

---

35. This story by Joseph Bruchac is reprinted here with his permission from the following source: Michael J. Caduto and Joseph Bruchac, *Keepers of the Earth: Native American Stories and Environmental Activities for Children.* Golden, CO: Fulcrum, 1989.

The first young man realized she was a divine being, and his mind was filled with good and beautiful thoughts. But the second young man only saw her as a beautiful young woman, and his mind filled with bad and desirous thoughts. As she came close to them, he reached out to grab at her. As soon as he did, there was the sound of thunder and a flash of lightning. The young man was covered by a cloud. When it cleared away, there was nothing left but a skeleton.

Then White Buffalo Calf Woman spoke clearly and directly. "Go to your people," she said, holding up the bundle in her hands so that the remaining young man could see it. "Tell your people that what I bring is a good thing. It is a holy gift to your nation, a message from the Buffalo People. Put up a medicine lodge for me and make it ready. I will come after four days have passed."

The young man followed her directions. He went back to his people and told them the message of the White Buffalo Calf Woman. The crier went through the camp and told everyone that something sacred was coming and all things should be made ready. They built the medicine lodge and made an earth altar that faced the west.

After four days had passed, the people saw something coming toward them. As it came closer, they saw that it was the White Buffalo Calf Woman. In her hands she carried the bundle as well as a cluster of sacred sage plant. The people welcomed her into the medicine lodge and gave her the seat of honor. She sat down slowly, peacefulness emanating from her being. Slowly she unwrapped the bundle and showed them what was inside. It was the sacred pipe. She held it up and explained the meaning of the sacred pipe.

"The bowl of the pipe," she said, "is made of red stone. It represents the flesh and blood of the Buffalo People and all other peoples. The wooden stem of the pipe symbolizes the plants and trees, and all living, growing, green things of this sacred earth. The smoke that passes through this pipe is the sacred wind, the breath that carries prayers up to Wakan Tanka, the Creator."

When she finished showing them the pipe, she then taught the people how to hold it and how to offer it to the earth and sky and the four sacred directions. She told them a great many things to remember.

"The sacred pipe," said the White Buffalo Calf Woman, "will show you the Good Red Road. When you follow this Good Red Road it will take you in the right direction." She smiled at the people gathered in the medicine lodge, then stood up and said, "Now I will leave, but you will see me again."

She left the lodge and the people followed her outside. She began to walk toward the setting sun and as the people watched, they saw her stop and roll once on the earth. When she stood again, she was a black buffalo. She walked along farther, then rolled again on the earth. This time she stood up and was a brown buffalo. Again she walked farther, again she rolled on the earth. She stood up as a red buffalo. Finally, a fourth time, she walked farther, rolled again, and stood up as a white buffalo calf. She continued to walk as a white buffalo calf until she disappeared into the horizon.

As soon as the White Buffalo Calf Woman was gone, herds of buffalo appeared around the camp. Now the people could hunt the buffalo, and they gave thanks with the sacred pipe for all the blessings. As long as they followed the Good Red Road of the sacred pipe and remembered what the White Buffalo Calf Woman had taught them, that all things were as connected as parts of the pipe, they lived happily and well.

GLOSSARY

altar: A specific spot that holds sacred space, usually on a table, rock, or other flat surface. Here offerings, candles, images, and art can be placed to honor certain energies, ancestors, the directions, and/or deities.

ancestor: Often an elder who has passed on, but can also be any friend or relative who has died and who has a connection with the living. This person may appear in dreams or omens and provide guidance. Traditional cultures give offerings to their ancestors to honor the dead who have gone before us.

archetype: An energetic imprint that lives within the collective unconscious and carries specific qualities, such as priestess, mother, teacher. Archetypes are portrayed in myths and big stories and can influence the way we relate to the world.

bodhisattva: A person or awakened being who vows to forgo enlightenment until all beings have reached enlightenment as well. This person is concerned for the well-being of all sentient beings and has achieved a high level of compassion, love, and wisdom; a love archetype of the sacred feminine.

calling the circle: To create a sacred space during ceremony by invoking and giving offerings to the four cardinal directions, above, below, and center.

ceremony: A tool of the sacred feminine used to create specific intentions, clearing, or manifesting and can be done in rhythm of the moon cycles or earth seasons.

consort: An external lover, partner, or friend whom one is connected to through sexual-spiritual activity; a love archetype of the sacred feminine.

crone: A woman who has passed through menopause and is holding the wisdom of age; an elder woman; a wisdom archetype of the sacred feminine.

dark mother: The eternal goddess; the creatrix or creative feminine source of all things. Many myths prior to the rising patriarchy of 2000 BCE figure a dark, wet, wild, creative mother goddess. Also a distinct connection to our ancestors and the first mother, such as Lucy, and our origins in Africa.

directions: Four cardinal or compass directions of east, south, west, and north which are used to create a sacred space or circle in ceremony; also often included are above, below, and center. Wherever we are on earth, we stand within a circle of directions and can tap into our personal sacred space.

elements: Four main elements of earth, air, fire, and water used in ceremony and associated with the four cardinal directions. These associations vary, but for this book we often used air for east, fire for south, water for west, and earth for north. Also connected to the processes in our body and on the earth.

fire bearer: A person who carries the wisdom and power of fire, associated with transformation and rebirth; a power archetype of the sacred feminine.

full moon: The time of the month when the moon is fully lit up in the sky; a time to honor abundance, make wishes, and celebrate growth.

goddess: A feminine archetype who figures in myth and holds certain qualities of power, love, and/or wisdom in the sacred feminine path.

guardian spirit: An animal guide of non-ordinary reality that one meets during dreams or journeys; also known as a power animal and can be a totem, personal medicine, or seasonal guide.

guide: A being of non-ordinary reality who helps on the spiritual plane.

healer: A person who supports and nurtures oneself as well as others; a love archetype of the sacred feminine.

initiate: Someone who has passed through a difficult experience such as giving birth, facing death, illness, or divorce *and* reclaimed the power of this event; a power archetype of the sacred feminine.

intention: A specific focus or goal for a ceremony, practice, or any creative endeavor.

menopause: The time during cessation of menses and afterwards; a time of holding in the blood and becoming a wise elder in the sacred feminine.

menses: Period or blood flow each month; a small death or initiation of power and a time of enhanced intuition, psychic perception, and dreams in the path of the sacred feminine.

myth: An epic story that features archetypes who provide insight into the deeper mysteries of human consciousness. A tool of the sacred feminine to reframe the stories we tell ourselves and enable us to better relate with the world using power, love, and wisdom.

new moon: The time of the month when the moon is invisible from the sky. A time to clear away things we want to let go of and plant new seeds of intention.

non-ordinary reality: A term used originally by Carlos Castaneda to define the shamanic or altered state of perception that is unbound by form or time. This is the realm of astral travel, dreams, psychic vision, and the journey work used in this book.

offering: Both an action and an item that is being offered. This is a ceremonial action to give water, flowers, incense, etc., and helps to honor the spirits as well as open the heart in generosity.

oracle: A method of divining to better understand relevant issues in one's life as well as provide lessons that are being learned; some examples of oracles are runes, tarot cards, the I Ching, reading tea leaves.

priestess: A woman who is capable of leading ceremony and assisting others in life transitions, and who has a strong connection to inner wisdom; a wisdom archetype of the sacred feminine.

reclaiming: A process of bringing to light buried stories and truths of the sacred feminine as well as the personal process of reframing negative or traumatic experiences so that they become experiences of power, love, and/or wisdom.

sacred feminine: The path of divine being in the shape of a woman; the process of honoring women, feminine gifts, female power, love, and wisdom as sacred or divine. Seeing divinity as the goddess equal to and in consort with the god.

waning moon: The time of the month when the moon is getting smaller, moving toward a new moon; a time to let go of old habits or things and release emotional stagnancy.

warrioress: A person who acts from a place of fearlessness and courage and understands setting clear boundaries; a power archetype of the sacred feminine.

waxing moon: The time of the month when the moon is becoming larger and moving toward full; a time to call in protection and start new projects as well as bless projects that are underway; also a good time to weed the garden so weeds don't continue to grow into fullness.

weaver: A person who knits together new ideas, thoughts, projects, and creative efforts. Someone who is involved with different aspects of the community and is able to see one's own place in the web of life; a wisdom archetype of the sacred feminine.

ACKNOWLEDGMENTS

This book was an immense journey, and the people who have helped see this book into form are numerous. Firstly, I am in great awe of all the women of my life, the women and goddesses of India and Hawai'i, and my feminine ancestors who directly spoke to me as I worked on this book. I am forever grateful to the land and Pele of Hawai'i for their beauty, spirit, and source of immense inspiration.

I am full of gratitude for my daughter, Yoko Mojave Lotus, who reminds me to be compassionate and to inspire her to become the best woman she can. I thank my parents for their endless support: my mother for her incredible wisdom which she has given me, and my father who taught me so much. I am also grateful for the connection that I hold with my grandmothers, both when they were alive and even now, in their spirit forms. I am thankful to my sister, Carmen Beth Koda, for her wisdom and clarity that remind me not to always take myself so seriously.

I am deeply grateful to Jill Walton, whose imminent guidance, foresight, and intuition helped form this entire book into being. Without her as both a reflection and co-teacher in our sacred feminine workshops, this work simply would not have been as rich as it is. I also thank our entire class for they provided a goldmine of women's experiences which helped me to shape this book.

I am also immensely thankful for the tireless work of my editor, Carrie Obry, who was a persistent and optimistic guide throughout this process. Her indefatigable feedback was crucial to bringing this book to a broad audience of women, and I cannot thank her enough for her patience.

Many times throughout this process I felt completely swamped by utter chaos, and I am thankful to my husband, Leon French, for being a constant support and endless supply of mirthfulness. I am also filled with gratitude for my dear friend Desiree Mwalimu, who is a constant inspiration as well as a clear and powerful woman holding the immensity of the sacred feminine in her life.

I wish to specifically thank Naomi Doumbia, Amina Meineker, Jamaica Johnston-Hancock, Amy Nemec, Samantha Shasenaye Elliot, White Eagle, and all the wondrous women in my life who both directly and indirectly inspired my work and are consistently working to create a sacred feminine reality. Their voices, their vision, their power, love, and wisdom are the community that is threaded throughout this book.

And lastly, I am so deeply thankful to be an American woman who has the freedom to write for the women of America and the world. I can only hope that this offering will inspire women to inspire women so that we may truly regain our power, love, and wisdom and find balance and harmony with the earth once again.

Resources

Books

Adovasio, J. M., Olga Soffer, and Jake Page. *The Invisible Sex: Uncovering the True Roles of Women in Prehistory*. New York: HarperCollins, 2007.

Austen, Hallie Iglehart. *The Heart of the Goddess: Art, Myth and Meditations of the World's Sacred Feminine*. Berkeley, CA: Wingbow Press, 1990.

Beckwith, Martha. *Hawaiian Mythology*. Honolulu: University of Hawaii Press, 1970.

Birnbaum, Lucia Chiavola. *Dark Mother: African Origins and Godmothers*. Lincoln, NE: Author's Choice Press, 2001.

———. *She Is Everywhere!: An Anthology of Writing in Womanist/ Feminist Spirituality*. Berkeley, CA: Belladonna, iUniverse, 2005.

Blofeld, John. *Bodhisattva of Compassion: The Mystical Tradition of Quan Yin*. Boulder, CO: Shambhala Publications, 1978.

Bonheim, Jalaja. *Aphrodite's Daughters: Women's Sexual Stories and the Journey of the Soul*. New York: Fireside, 1997.

Brown, Joseph Epes (recorder and editor). *The Sacred Pipe: Black Elk's Account of the Seven Rites of the Oglala Sioux*. Norman: University of Oklahoma Press, 1953.

Budapest, Zsuzsanna E. *The Grandmother of Time: A Woman's Book of Celebrations, Spells and Sacred Objects for Every Month of the Year*. New York: HarperCollins, 1989.

———. *Summoning the Fates: A Woman's Guide to Destiny*. New York: Harmony, 1998.

Budge, E. A. Wallis. *The Gods of the Egyptians: Studies in Egyptian Mythology*, 2 vols. New York: Dover Publications, 1969.

———. *Osiris and the Egyptian Resurrection*, 2 vols. New York: Dover Publications, 1973.

Cabot, Laurie, with Tom Cowan. *Power of the Witch: The Earth, the Moon and the Magical Path to Enlightenment*. New York : Delta, Bantam Doubleday Dell Publishing, 1989.

Caduto, Michael J., and Joseph Bruchac. *Keepers of the Earth: Native American Stories and Environmental Activities for Children*. Golden, CO: Fulcrum, 1989.

Callan, Dawn. *Awakening the Warrior Within: Secrets of Personal Safety and Inner Security*. Ukia, CA: Tenacity Press, 1999.

Campbell, Joseph. *The Hero with a Thousand Faces*. New York: Princeton University Press, 1973.

Campbell, Joseph, with Bill Moyers and Betty Sue Flowers, editor. *The Power of Myth*. New York: Doubleday, 1988.

Cashford, Jules, and Anne Baring. *The Myth of the Goddess: Evolution of an Image*. London: Arkana, Penguin Books, 1993.

Ching, Linda. *Hawaiian Goddesses*. Honolulu: Hawaiian Goddesses Publishing, 1987.

Christ, Carol P. *Odyssey with the Goddess: A Spiritual Quest in Crete*. New York: Continuum Publishing, 1995.

Conway, D. J. *Maiden, Mother, Crone*. St. Paul, MN: Llewellyn Publications, 2003.

Daly, Mary. *Gyn/ecology: The Metaethics of Radical Feminism*. Boston: Beacon Press, 1990.

Davis, Elizabeth, and Carol Leonard. *The Woman's Wheel of Life*. New York: Viking Arkana, 1996.

Davis-Kimball, Jeannine. *Warrior Women: An Archaeologist's Search for History's Hidden Heroines*. New York: Warner Books, 2002.

Diamant, Anita. *The Red Tent*. New York: Picador, 1997.

Dimmitt, Cornelia, and J. A. B. van Buitenen. *Classical Hindu Mythology: A Reader in the Sanskrit Puranas*. Philadelphia: Temple University Press, 1978.

Doumbia, Adama and Naomi. *The Way of the Elders: West African Spirituality and Tradition*. St. Paul, MN: Llewellyn Worldwide, 2004.

Duncan, Lois. *The Magic of Spider Woman*. New York: Scholastic, 1996.

Eisler, Riane. *The Chalice and the Blade: Our History, Our Future*. San Francisco: HarperCollins, 1995.

———. *Sacred Pleasure*. New York: HarperCollins, 1995.

Elter, Cynthia. *Living in the Lap of the Goddess: The Feminist Spirituality Movement in America*. Boston: Beacon Press Books, 1995.

Estés, Clarissa Pinkola. *Women Who Run with the Wolves: Myths and Stories of the Wild Woman Archetype*. New York: Ballantine Books, 1995.

Feurstein, Georg. *Tantra: The Path of Ecstasy*. Boston: Shambhala Publications, 1998.

Frawley, David. *Tantric Yoga and the Wisdom Goddesses: Spiritual Secrets of Ayurveda*. Salt Lake City, UT: Passage Press, 1994.

Galland, China. *Longing for Darkness: Tara and the Black Madonna*. New York: Viking Penguin, 2007.

George, Christopher S. *The Candamaharosana Tantra, Chapters 1–8: A Critical and English Translation*. American Oriental Series, no. 56. New Haven, CT: American Oriental Society, translated 1974.

George, Demetra. *Mysteries of the Dark Moon: The Healing Power of the Dark Goddess*. San Francisco: HarperSanFrancisco, 1992.

———. *The Civilization of the Goddess: The World of Old Europe*. San Francisco: HarperSanFrancisco, 1991.

Gimbutas, Marija. Foreword by Joseph Campbell. *The Language of the Goddess*. San Francisco: HarperSanFrancisco, 1989.

Hancock, Graham. *Supernatural: Meetings with the Ancient Teachers of Mankind*. New York: The Disinformation Co., 2007.

Harkless, Necia Desiree. *Heart to Heart*. Lexington, KY: Heart to Heart and Associates, 1995.

Harner, Michael. *The Way of the Shaman*. New York: HarperCollins, 1990.

Hathaway, Nancy. *The Friendly Guide to Mythology: A Mortal's Companion to the Fantastical Realm of Gods, Goddesses, Monsters and Heroes*. New York: Penguin Group, 2001.

Husain, Shahrukh. *Living Wisdom: The Goddess*. Alexandria, VA: Time-Life Books, 1997.

Kenyon, Tom, and Judi Sion. *The Magdalen Manuscript: The Alchemies of Horus and the Sex Magic of Isis*. Boulder, CO: Sounds True, 2006.

Kidd, Sue Monk. *The Dance of the Dissident Daughter: A Woman's Journey from Christian Tradition to the Sacred Feminine*. New York: HarperCollins, 1996.

Kinstler, Clysta. *The Moon Under Her Feet*. New York: HarperCollins, 1989.

L'Engle, Madeleine. *A Wrinkle in Time*. New York: Square Fish, Macmillan, 1962.

Marashinsky, Amy Sophia, illustrated by Hrana Janto. *The Goddess Oracle: A Way to Wholeness through the Goddess and Ritual*. Boston: Element Books, 1997.

Marvelly, Paula. *Women of Wisdom: A Journey of Enlightenment by Women of Vision through the Ages*. London: Watkins Publishing, 2005.

Mascetti, Manuela Dunn. *The Song of Eve: Mythology and Symbols of the Goddess*. New York: Fireside, Simon and Schuster, 1990.

Monaghan, Patricia. *The Goddess Path: Myths, Invocations and Rituals*. St. Paul, MN: Llewellyn Publications, 2000.

Muktananda, Swami. *Nawa Yogini Tantra: Yoga for Women*. Munger, Bihar, India: Yoga Publications Trust, Bihar School of Yoga, 1983.

Murdock, Maureen. *The Heroine's Journey*. Boston: Shambhala Publications, 1990.

Noble, Vicki. *Shakti Woman: Feeling Our Fire, Healing Our World*. San Francisco: HarperCollins, 1991.

Northrop, Christiane. *Women's Bodies, Women's Wisdom: Creating Physical and Emotional Health and Healing*. New York: Random House, 2010.

Perera, Sylvia Brinton. *Descent to the Goddess: A Way of Initiation for Women*. Toronto: Inner City Books, 1981.

Ragan, Kathleen. *Fearless Girls, Wise Women and Beloved Sisters: Heroines in Folktales from Around the World*. New York: W.W. Norton & Co., 1998.

Redmond, Layne. *When the Drummers Were Women: A Spiritual History of Rhythm*. New York: Three Rivers Press, 1997.

Rinpoche, Sogyal. *The Tibetan Book of Living and Dying*. San Francisco: HarperSanFrancisco, 2002.

Sams, Jamie. *The 13 Original Clan Mothers*. New York: HarperCollins, 1993.

San Souci, Robert D., illustrated by Brian Pinkney. *Sukey and the Mermaid*. New York: Aladdin Paperbacks, 1992.

Schulz, Mona Lisa. *The New Feminine Brain: How Women Can Develop Their Inner Strengths, Genius, and Intuition*. New York: Free Press, 2005.

Simmer-Brown, Judith. *Dakini's Warm Breath: The Feminine Principle in Tibetan Buddhism*. Boston: Shambhala Publications, 2001

Sjöö, Monica, and Barbara Mor. *The Great Cosmic Mother: Rediscovering the Religion of the Earth*. San Francisco: Harper & Row, 1987.

Starhawk. *Dreaming the Dark: Magic, Sex and Politics*. Boston: Beacon Press, 1982.

Starhawk, and Hilary Valentine. *The Twelve Wild Swans: A Journey to the Realm of Magic, Healing and Action*. San Francisco: HarperSanFrancisco, 2000.

Stark, Marcia. *The Dark Goddess: Dancing with the Shadow*. Freedom, CA: The Crossing Press, 1993.

Stone, Merlin. *Ancient Mirrors of Womanhood: A Treasury of Goddess and Heroine Lore from Around the World*. Boston: Beacon Press, 1979, 1991.

———. *When God Was a Woman*. New York: Barnes & Noble, Bantam Doubleday Dell, 1976.

Stubbs, Kenneth Ray, ed. *Women of the Light: The New Sacred Prostitute*. Larkspur, CA: Secret Garden, 1994.

Tisdale, Sallie. *Women of the Way: Discovering 2,500 Years of Buddhist Wisdom*. San Francisco: HarperCollins, 2006.

Villoldo, Alberto, and Erik Jedresen. *Dance of the Four Winds*. Rochester, VT: Destiny Books, 1995.

Walker, Barbara G. *The Woman's Encyclopedia of Myths and Secrets*. San Francisco: HarperCollins, 1983.

———. *The Woman's Dictionary of Symbols and Sacred Objects*. San Francisco: HarperCollins, 1988.

Williamson, Marianne. *A Woman's Worth*. New York: Ballantine Books, 1993.

Woolger, Jennifer Barker, and Roger J. *The Goddess Within: A Guide to the Eternal Myths that Shape Women's Lives*. New York: Fawcett Columbine, Ballantine Books, 1989.

Websites

CARE: www.care.org

Global Fund for Women: www.globalfundforwomen.org

Spiral Muse: www.spiralmuse.com

Articles

Bird, Stephanie Rose. "Summer Water Rites," July 19, 2007, www.llewellyn.com/journal/article/652. Retrieved on January 29, 2011.

Collie, El. "Branded by the Spirit," from *Shared Transformation*. www.elcollie.com. Retrieved on July 12, 2009.

Doumbia, Naomi. "African Goddess: Mother of Shadow and Light," from Lucia Chiavola Birnbaum, *She Is Everywhere!: An Anthology of Writing in Womanist/Feminist Spirituality*. Berkeley, CA: Belladonna, iUniverse, 2005.

Hartmann, Diana Rose. "Sacred Prostitutes," www.moondance.org/1997/summer97/nonfiction/sacred.htm. Retrieved on October 15, 2009.

Jennet, Dianne E. "Menstruating Women/Menstruating Goddesses: Sites of Sacred Power in Kerala, South India, Sangam Era (100–500 CE) to the Present." www.metaformia.org. Retrieved on June 12, 2010.

Karimi, Faith. "South African Doctor Invents Female Condoms with Teeth to Prevent Rape," http://articles.cnn.com/2010-06 -20/world/south.africa.female.condom. Retrieved on January 29, 2011.

Kristof, Nicholas D., and Sheryl WuDunn. "The Women's Crusade," *New York Times Magazine*, August 23, 2009, pp. 28–39.

Marler, Joan. "Goddesses of Old Europe, Part II," *Sonoma County Women's Voices*, no. 94, November 1989, pp. 1, 7.

———. "Interview with Marija Gimbutas." *Sonoma County Women's Voices*, no. 94, November 1989, pp. 1, 6, 12.

Parameswaran, Devanayagi. May 4, 2009, 9:25am, on *"Tantra: From Om to Orgasm,"* www.humanityhealing.ning.com.

Scott, David C. "Radha in the Erotic Play of the Universe," www .religion-online.org/showarticle.asp?title=146. Retrieved December 12, 2009.

Tharoor, Ishaan. "12,000-Year-Old Shaman Unearthed in Israel," *Time* magazine, November 11, 2008, www.time.com/time /world/article/0,8599,1858121,00.html. Retrieved January 29, 2011.

Thorn, Thorskegga, "Spinning in Myths and Folktales," www.thorshof .org/spinmyth.htm. Retrieved on September 30, 2009.

SACRED PATH OF REIKI
Healing as a Spiritual Discipline
KATALIN KODA

This unique guidebook combines traditional Reiki techniques with chakra healing, the magical arts, and the author's own spiritual and clairvoyant experience. Reiki Master Katalin Koda has studied Tibetan Buddhism, practiced Kundalini yoga, and researched ancient Vedic knowledge of the human energy field in India. The result is a powerful new way to practice Reiki, a holistic spiritual approach that Koda calls the Reiki Warrior path.

The way of the warrior has long been used by indigenous cultures to cultivate discipline and responsibility. By fusing this age-old tradition with a modern healing art and the story of her own journey, Koda offers a powerful, one-of-a-kind approach to help Reiki practitioners come into their own as skilled, compassionate, and well-balanced healers.

Sacred Path of Reiki presents tested theories and original practices that demonstrate how to develop Reiki into an integrated healing system and transcendent spiritual path. It will appeal to both Reiki students and teachers.

ISBN-13: 978-0-7387-1445-5
7 ¹/₂ x 9 ¹/₈, 240 pp. $19.95

GODDESS ALOUD!
Transforming Your World Through Rituals & Mantras
MICHELLE SKYE

Michelle Skye presents a unique guide to connecting with goddess energy through the power of your voice and achieving spiritual fulfillment and empowerment. Featuring 27 goddesses from diverse cultures around the world, this practical guide provides simple yet effective mantras and rituals to help you attune to each goddess for peace, a healthier environment, forgiveness, love, self-love, healing, growth, hope, and spirituality.

Draw love to you with Freyja, Norse goddess of passion and sex; practice forgiveness with Arianrhod, Welsh sovereign lady; and celebrate your feminine power with Isis, Egyptian goddess of magic and motherhood.

ISBN-13: 978-0-7387-1442-4
7 ¹/₂ x 9 ¹/₈, 264 pp.   **$18.95**

To order, call 1-877-NEW-WRLD
Prices subject to change without notice
Order at Llewellyn.com 24 hours a day, 7 days a week!

The Goddess Guide

Exploring the Attributes and Correspondences of the Divine Feminine

Priestess Brandi Auset

Which goddess will help me invite love into my life? Is there an Indian goddess who presides over wealth? Does Kuan Yin represent compassion or truth?

For anyone who's ever wondered which form of the Divine Feminine to invoke for a particular ritual, blessing, prayer, or meditation, The Goddess Guide is a goddess-send! As the first and only book of its kind on the market today, this invaluable at-a-glance cross-reference offers instant info on more than 400 goddesses from diverse cultures around the world—simply look up the keyword that best matches your intention.

The goddesses are organized according to their names, attributes, colors, elements, sabbats, light and dark feminine aspects (maidens, mothers, and crones), and geographical regions. Get to know all aspects of the goddesses who bring about healing, heightened passion, success, weight loss, and much more. This reference book deserves a spot on every serious practitioner's bookshelf.

ISBN-13: 978-0-7387-1551-3

6 x 9, 336 pp. $16.95

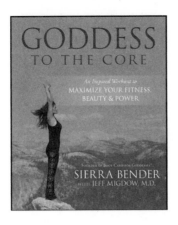

GODDESS TO THE CORE
An Inspired Workout to Maximize Your Fitness, Beauty & Power
SIERRA BENDER WITH JEFF MIGDOW, M.D.

Everybody these days is buzzing about "body, mind, and spirit," but no one has put the pieces together into a complete, powerful, life-changing experience the way that Sierra Bender has.

Goddess to the Core will transform you into a complete, self-assured, and well-balanced goddess. With a broad base of practical tools and spiritual inspiration, Bender gives you a workout for all four of your bodies: physical, mental, emotional, and spiritual. Experience how these bodies have "muscles," and discover how neglecting them can lead to disharmony and ill health. With Bender's "inside-out workout," you will learn to sculpt these four bodies. By empowering, balancing, and working out each one, you will claim your worth, take command of your space, sculpt your shape, and balance your emotions and your mind while remaining in your true spiritual center—the Goddess within.

ISBN-13: 978-0-7387-1503-2
7 $^1/_2$ x 9 $^1/_8$, 336 pp. $21.95